BUILT FOR CHANGE

"Shiva the Nataraj—the Cosmic Dancer." From 7th-century India, this image shows the Hindu concepts of creation, preservation and destruction. In business as in life, each must have its place. (Image Courtesy www.exoticindia.com.)

BUILT FOR CHANGE

Essential Traits of
Transformative Companies

T. D. KLEIN

 PRAEGER

AN IMPRINT OF ABC-CLIO, LLC
Santa Barbara, California • Denver, Colorado • Oxford, England

Library of Congress Cataloging-in-Publication Data

Klein, T. D. (Todd David)
 Built for change : essential traits of transformative companies / T.D. Klein.
     p. cm.
 Includes bibliographical references and index.
  ISBN 978-0-313-38142-3 (hard copy : alk. paper) — ISBN 978-0-313-38143-0 (ebook)
 1. Organizational change.   2. Industrial management—Case studies.   3. Organizational effectiveness.   I. Title.
  HD58.8.K569   2010
  658.4'06—dc22   2010029016

ISBN: 978-0-313-38142-3
EISBN: 978-0-313-38143-0

14 13 12 11 10   1 2 3 4 5

This book is also available on the World Wide Web as an eBook.
Visit www.abc-clio.com for details.

Praeger
An Imprint of ABC-CLIO, LLC

ABC-CLIO, LLC
130 Cremona Drive, P.O. Box 1911
Santa Barbara, California 93116-1911

This book is printed on acid-free paper ∞

Manufactured in the United States of America

To dinner guest #14, with gratitude

CONTENTS

Preface   ix

Acknowledgments   xiii

1. Overview   1

2. Universality   11

3. Fearlessness   23

4. Process   35

5. Irreverence   49

6. Banishing Small Thinking   63

7. Appetite for Destruction   75

8. Detachment   85

9. Reinvention   95

10. Becoming *Built for Change*   107

Bibliography   111

Index   127

PREFACE

As an early-stage venture capitalist, my job is like one long, protracted, poker night. Every move my partners and I make is a gamble—whether to hold or raise, play another hand or cash in. Indeed, to manage a portfolio of startup investments is to play 10 or 15 hands of five-card draw simultaneously. You have to ante up to get in the game. If you want to see more cards, you are expected to toss in some more chips. Call the bluffs, go for the high hand, and draw to the inside straight—that's how you win.

But my odds are better than in poker. Perhaps a third of my portfolio folds completely, another third puts me a little ahead or a little behind, and the final third wins big, sometimes very big, and that's what keeps the game going.

When I filled out the application to business school nearly 20 years ago, one of the essay questions was "What aspect of yourself would you like to develop or improve?" I answered that I wanted to be clairvoyant, figuring that even if I never developed paranormal skills, the answer might at least make me memorable to the admissions committee. Evidently it did, because I got in. While I never learned to see into the future or read people's minds, after graduation and some 15 years helping companies plan for growth, I eventually did develop a venture capitalist's most important skill—pattern recognition—and what follows is a description of those patterns. Unfortunately, I'm still working on clairvoyance. I still can't spot a losing hand before I've anted up.

So, what are the signs that the biggest of the big winners show? What skills and traits can be seen from the very earliest days of a new enterprise, if you're looking for them? A certain fearlessness, an unusually clear sense of what the company does (and what it doesn't do), a detached willingness to self-critique, and a genuine zeal for reinvention: these are just four of the eight characteristics we'll explore in this book.

Time and time again the standout business enterprise that strongly exhibits one or more of these traits proves to be what I call a transformative company—either in terms of what it does or how it does it, or, often, both.

These companies are *built for change;* they are born of change, motivated by change, and yet are somehow oblivious to change. They alter the direction of industries or often create new ones. They have an internal structure and wisdom that is theirs and theirs alone. They pride themselves on a workplace culture that is often different, maybe even unusual. Talented people do not merely gravitate toward these enterprises; they leap barriers and make sacrifices to get there. Furthermore, as these bold company builders stare down risks that would cause others to lose their nerve, they change the entire market's assessment of what is possible.

Transformative, *built for change* companies are cropping up all over the world. When college students from the United States and elsewhere were asked recently where in the world to find opportunity, the United States ranked third, behind the United Kingdom and China. Accordingly, it should surprise no one if the next Google or Amazon or UPS comes from one of these countries or from another high-ranking contender such as India, Australia, or France. Companies that are *built for change* recruit worldwide, partner worldwide, source resources worldwide, and welcome a diversity of ideas and cultures to their global businesses.

Will we recognize tomorrow's winners as they emerge? I believe we will as long as we scrutinize the signs—the characteristics that indicate transformation ahead. This book is aimed at explaining—for the first time—what being *built for change* really looks like, wherever we may find it. To best understand the concept, we need to be willing to draw upon many different traditions, cultural references, and experiences. To illustrate my point, let me tell you a story. It's at the heart of how this book came to be.

"HOW COULD THERE BE A GOOGLE?"

"It doesn't make any sense—how could there be a Google?" the baffled Indian, a Mumbai native, asked me. We were attending a dinner at the Young Presidents' Organization's annual Global Leadership Conference in Cape Town, South Africa.

My questioner was the scion of a merchant family that had built one of the largest construction companies in the world. To a person whose milieu is strictly concrete and steel, where things are built step by step, phenomenal growth and an ephemeral product just didn't compute. How can there be a Google?

I answered him using the Western lexicon of entrepreneurial risk taking and capital formation. I credited academic preparation and the venture-friendly ecosystem of the Silicon Valley—Stanford University, Sand Hill Road, Wilson Sonsini. And I got nowhere.

"Yes," he said, looking frustrated, "but what makes Google different from all the rest?"

I thought for a moment and began to realize that his lack of understanding was not technical or economic; he just couldn't *see* what I was talking about. So, after confirming that he was a practicing Hindu, I recalled the ubiquitous image of Shiva, a god as familiar to Hindus as Buddha is to Buddhists. In particular, I asked him to conjure the dancing Shiva of Nataraj, a figure from the seventh century AD that nearly one billion Hindus contemplate to consider how best to live their lives. I wanted my listener to consider the fact that the same image could well depict Google and its success. In short, I asked him to think of Google as a Shiva company.

The details of that image and what the various parts of it could be construed to represent will play a supporting role in the book you are about to read. For now, let me say only that I was taken aback by how powerfully resonant and emblematic Shiva was for my dinner companion. When I finished, he sat for a moment agape. "To think," he marveled, "that I had to fly to Africa in order to meet someone from Washington D.C., who would explain to me my own cultural history so that I might understand what I considered to be unexplainable!" Google now made perfect sense to him.

In the months that followed, I realized that our conversation had, inadvertently, taught me something new. I saw that the image of a dancing Shiva well reflected the most transformative aspects of several of our company's greatest portfolio winners, as well as many of today's economic wonders. I looked at business superstars such as Dell, Southwest Airlines, and Starbucks, and I found that the Shiva metaphor held up well as a model for transformative business. It became my shadow as I began to articulate the characteristics of transformation.

With this ancient image in mind, I started considering prospective investments differently, questioning whether each had the traits of what I was then thinking of as "a Shiva company." Many of them did, but others that possessed the traditional attributes of success—things like management track record and significant market size—fell short when measured against my new metrics. Uncannily, these were also the companies with the most disappointing long-term performance.

Over time, I've realized that there are ineffable qualities that allow companies to outpace the competition and create extraordinary value in a short period of time. Of course, you don't have to be Hindu for the Shiva image to provide a template for recognizing and describing the characteristics of companies that are *built for change*. I'm not. However, you do have to open your mind to other modes of thought, unfamiliar cultural symbology, and nontraditional ways of describing business attributes.

In this book I will share my insights into some of the most extraordinary companies in recent memory. As you will discover, there are many ways to be transformative and a variety of definitions for what it means to be *built for change*. The framework I present is not intended to help you cope with the short-term gyrations of the stock market, but it may make you a savvier investor, a more transformative entrepreneur or executive, or simply a more discerning employee. What's more, it may just provide you with a new kind of mental image when you think about a company's success—one with four arms, a drum, a dwarf, and a gracefully upturned hand—because, no matter what form they take, we all want to be associated with transformative companies.

ACKNOWLEDGMENTS

Many people have provided encouragement and inspiration throughout the preparation of this manuscript, particularly several of my close friends and associates in Young Presidents' Organization (YPO). Every day I learn something new from them, and being part of YPO has been one of the most rewarding experiences of my life. I'd especially like to mention Michael Gottdenker, Devin Schain, Nelson Carbonell, Ed Bagdasarian, Rob Follows, Gadi Kaufmann, Jeff Handy, Todd Foreman, Brooke Coburn, Todd Kaplan, Larry Weinberg, and Fred Schaufeld.

My YPO forum plays a unique role in my life, and Michelle Boggs, Dave Donahower, Dan Rowe, Mark Michael, Willy Walker, and particularly Rob Granader have given me unqualified support and guidance as I've worked on this project. Thanks for your patience and encouragement.

Charles Steiner has been a friend, mentor, guru, and inspiration to me on a personal and professional level for my entire life. He sets the standard for integrity, entrepreneurial vision, abiding generosity, and the capacity to see opportunity in every situation. When I consider every wise decision I've ever made or disastrous choice I've narrowly avoided, inevitably each was preceded by a conversation with Chuck. And, as the apple doesn't fall far from the tree, Chuck's sons, Adam and Brian, have been thoughtful partners and close personal friends since before we all could walk.

Thanks go to Ellen Wojahn, one of the most demanding researchers and writing partners a person could ask for. Ellen's imagination, energy, and fundamental business acumen were essential to seeing this manuscript all the way through.

Richard Wolffe has been a friend, advisor and sagacious counselor to me throughout this process. Arriving in Washington as a cub reporter, he has managed to reach the pinnacle of his profession as a journalist, author, television analyst, and pundit with perfect equanimity and humility. In this town, that is truly a remarkable feat.

Of course, this book would not have been possible without the generous time given by the chairmen and CEOs whose stories represent the substance of the manuscript. Jim Koch, John Klein, Frank D'Souza, Eric Dunn, Alan Klapmeier, Herb Kelleher, Dan Nye, Dave Huber, Stanley Hainsworth, and Michael Chasen all shared thorough, candid, and comprehensive perspectives of their experiences as founders, executives, and leaders. This book is intended for the people they inspire every day.

Special recognition belongs to Verne Harnish, author of *Mastering the Rockefeller Habits*. Verne is many things to many people—author, consultant, renowned speaker, among others—but to me he is simply one of the best business educators of our generation. Like Peter Drucker, he has that singular ability to identify the most nuanced business concepts and to disaggregate, prioritize, and then present them in memorable and effective ways. Literally thousands of companies are better off today because of his wisdom, and, without his encouragement, this book would not have been written.

Andrew Sherman is one of the greatest teachers and authors on the subject of capital formation active today. He also happens to be a damn good deal attorney. Along with Andrew, Rich Chasen of Savvian is one of the anchors for the annual capital formation seminar that I chair. Together, they represent decades of transactional wisdom, and I learn from every encounter I have with them.

Many people have had a profound effect on my professional life, especially during my venture career. I am indebted to Jim Pastoriza, who is one of the most thoughtful and quietly forceful investors I've ever known, as well as his up-and-coming partner Joe Harar. Likewise, Neal Simon, Duncan Butler, Steve Czech, Mike Lincoln, Cal Simmons, and Don Baer have been mentors and advisors to me as Legend Ventures has taken flight. I only wish my friend and founding advisory board chairman Jack Valenti were here to enjoy this with us. I miss his wise counsel every day.

The executives of Legend's portfolio companies: Dave Spofford (Invoice Insight), Bruno Pati and Phil Wiser (Sezmi), Paul Hurley (ideeli), Eric Remer and Allan Wolff (PaySimple), Steven Bruny (Aztek), Mike Dager (Arxan), and Jeff Reedy (Overture Networks) inspire hundreds of people every day with their creativity and entrepreneurial passion. These are the true heroes of our economy—risk takers, dreamers, and doers. I also want to mention Bob Pavey and Gary Morganthaler (Morganthaler), Andy Lack (Bloomberg), Fred Bamber (Solstice), Lt. General Ken Minihan (Paladin), and Peter Meekin (Trident), each of whom represents the epitome of what board directors should be: engaged, thoughtful, informed, patient, and willing to do anything and everything to help their companies succeed. Finally, John Borthwick exemplifies the entrepreneurs' entrepreneur. He's whip-smart and

I always know what I'll be focused on in six months' time by looking at what he's doing now.

Special recognition belongs to Legend's founding shareholder group, who are composed of some of the savviest executives I've ever known: Alan Utay, Alan Meltzer, Marc Joseph, Cliff White, Tony Naylor, Davor Kapelina, Gary Jonas, Ron Kaplan, Rich Samet, Jami Van, Andy Fireman, Amena Ali, and Gus Bessalel.

The partners at Kinetic Ventures—Willie Heflin, Jake Tarr, and Nelson Chu—gave me my start in venture capital and understood that it is truly an apprenticeship business. I am forever grateful for the opportunity.

My friend Rob Moss has been a sustaining force in my life and has shown me what it means to be truly balanced. Similarly, Hillary and Frank Stiff and Eve Benton and Malcolm Bund have been enthusiastic supporters and dear friends for many years now. They've influenced my thinking and enriched my sense of life's possibilities.

Amy Quigley has been a friend, advisor, and partner. She somehow manages to maintain a strict sense of professionalism while being completely irreverent and hilarious. I'm not exactly sure how she does it, but if you ever have the chance to work on a project with her, do it and you'll be cracking up while still succeeding at whatever you have set out to do.

My family has been a constant source of support to me throughout this process, starting with my mother, Bonnie, and sister, Pam; each has encouraged me to try whatever came into my head with openness and possibility.

My children, Sarah, Jake, Zach, and Max, keep me grounded and remind me of the inherent bliss that comes from appreciating new experiences. They delight me daily with their humor, fascination, and joy.

My wife, Cindy, is my strongest advocate, most diplomatic critic, and closest confidante. She has supported me through tough career choices, difficult family matters, and personal challenges without number. She manages to pack more things into a single day than I could in a month. She is an inspiration to me and to our whole family. This book would not have been possible without her support and encouragement.

T. D. Klein
Washington, DC, March 2010

Chapter 1

OVERVIEW

This opening chapter presents a framework for what follows. It also provides a handy summary of the book's themes and basic assertions—either to help you prioritize which chapters to read or as a guide for you to refer to later.

First, a disclaimer. As mentioned in the Preface, the structure for this book is based on an ancient image of a celebrated Hindu god. But as you read, please remember this is not a book about religion. The image as it is presented here is a tool, a visual metaphor for a series of ideas related to innovation and transformation. It was chosen because of its breadth and because it represents a multicultural perspective that is both emblematic and essential in order to compete in our global economy.

So, if the image works for you and helps connect you to the book's underlying concepts, that's great. If you are able to reinterpret the concepts with a vocabulary of your own that holds greater personal resonance, so much the better. However, if the image distracts you from absorbing the messages of this book, then by all means, move past it. From the book's opening sentence to its final paragraph, the focus should remain on understanding transformational enterprises and what distinguishes them from other companies.

Now, straight to it: what constitutes a transformative company? What kind of companies are *built for change*?

Transformative companies are *built for change* because they use their transformative characteristics to generate extraordinary growth, stimulate innovation, attract and retain the most talented employees, and adapt to shifting circumstances. Because they know themselves and their businesses uncommonly well, and because they have worked hard to develop a specific outlook on how their people should meet the challenges of the marketplace, these companies are unusually well-situated to recognize and direct the unfolding of ever-present change.

What are these transformative characteristics? After 15 years as a venture capitalist, I can assure you that there is no Rosetta Stone readily available to decipher the secret code. Nevertheless, if you stay in the venture capital business long enough, you will start to recognize patterns. What you are about to read is a summary of those patterns as demonstrated by some of the most remarkable companies in recent memory. Some companies represent investments I have made, while others are ones I wished I'd made. But in all cases, the chapters of this book represent the sometimes inscrutable ways I try mentally to vet each of the hundreds of business plans that flow across my desk every year. After I have run through the standard venture tumbler of market size and growth rate, management team experience and domain expertise, I ask an entirely different set of questions about the founding business concept and the structure, culture, and capabilities of the company, specifically:

1. Is there something aspirational about the very concept of the company, something that will lend it *universality*?
2. Does it perceive risk in an unusual way with almost perfect customer knowledge, meeting competitive challenges in a way that is strikingly *fearless*?
3. Do its *processes* encourage creativity while allowing for rapid scaling?
4. Does the *irreverence* of its corporate culture attract and retain quality, self-motivated employees?
5. Do internal policies encourage innovation to bubble up from the bottom and allow the workforce to *banish small thinking*?
6. Does it approach its market opportunity and entrenched business models with an *appetite for destruction*?
7. Does the company appear able to step outside itself for periodic *detachment* and reflection?
8. If crisis or opportunity were to arise, could this company *reinvent itself*?

In the course of this book, we will examine these eight different traits that brand a company as transformative. The chapter titles categorize the primary characteristics of transformative companies and provide a map to the Shiva image that was the genesis of this book (see Preface.)

Here are a few things to keep in mind as you read:

- *Success alone doesn't make a company transformative.* The companies I cite influence other companies, their markets, and our shared global future, while others merely succeed in executing a business plan.
- *Being transformative is usually a transitory state of being.* Companies rarely stay transformative their entire lives.
- *Transformative companies are built for change.* This means they possess certain traits or capabilities that give them advantages over other

enterprises, especially in times of disruption or change. In his seminal book, Jim Collins speaks of companies that are *Built to Last*. The companies mentioned in this book may or may not endure, but for a time they are transformative, and if managed properly, they are more capable than their peers of weathering change.

- *Built for change companies may be transformative in just one way or in multiple ways.* A few stellar companies will qualify in several categories, so don't be surprised to see the likes of Amazon and Google being mentioned several times in this book.

- *Being transformative doesn't necessarily imply that a company is highly competitive or especially aggressive, though it may be.* In many respects, transformative companies are the ones least interested in what the competition is doing. They are immersed in what they themselves are doing and how to do it in the best way possible.

- *Nonetheless, this does not mean that a transformative company is unaware of the rest of the marketplace.* In fact, transformative companies have an uncanny or highly developed ability to take a clear external view of where markets are going. The result is a company that competes for a place in the market and for the consumer's enthusiastic acceptance, but rarely does it act or react strictly in response to the strategies and tactics of its competitors.

- *Transformative companies often have strong, creative leaders, but being transformative is not about charismatic leadership.* It is about management's creation, care, and pruning of a corporate culture that is well-suited not only to the personality of the founder but also to the idiosyncrasies of the company's products, services, and markets.

- *Finally, and most importantly, by asking the right questions and looking at your business in a new way,* you can emulate many if not all of these traits.

It might be tempting to say "This is all fine, but my company is not Google, so what good will this do me?" Granted, few have created an amazing search algorithm; however, the traits identified here appear in many types of businesses, old and new, high-tech and industrial. There are opportunities here for every company.

What follows is a brief, user-friendly summary of the transformative characteristics described in this book. There is also a challenge at the end to help jump-start your thinking about transforming your own business.

CHAPTER 2: UNIVERSALITY

As you start to read this book, you may wonder: Is there something at the headwaters of transformative companies that seems well beyond what is considered typically strategic or tactical? Is there anything that seems to suggest that the best way to become a transformative company is to be singularly aware of factors that others ignore? The answer is yes, via universality, so let's address it first.

Companies that I label transformative by dint of universality seem to be a perfect fit with the consuming public's wants and needs. Sometimes by luck, but usually by design, these companies have managed to tap into some of humankind's most elemental aspirations and motivations. Think of Google, which addresses human curiosity and is now synonymous with "search," or Facebook, where the one-word mission is to "connect." Other entrants have reached for success in the same niches, but these companies—and others such as LinkedIn (think "empowerment") and Starbucks("escape")—have been the ones to grab and hold the brass ring. Right place, right time, right people—yes, this is true in these cases, but delve deeper and you will see that there are ways in which these exemplars have cupped their universal human aims like a tiny flame, or blown in the right amount of oxygen to help them grow.

CHAPTER 3: FEARLESSNESS

To a company that displays its transformative energies through fearlessness, the barriers to entry don't look very high—even when they are actually towering over them. Perhaps the walls seem to be crumbling, even when they're not. Such a company goes forward undaunted with a sort of doughty brio that is a function of perceiving risk in a way that is totally unlike that of its competitors. With deep personal convictions and customer insight that is much more acute than its competitors, a fearless company sees the world differently.

When Blackboard launched its effort to bring professors into a digital world of online assignments and grading, its founders were aware that this group was not known for its early adoption. Yet somehow that potential barrier was less visible than the opportunity that awaited the company to bring education to its students in the online world they inhabited. As Blackboard's founders expressed it, they *couldn't not* go forward.

Another company founded on a can't-lose estimation of the market is Cirrus Aviation, the makers of the world's most popular aircraft in private aviation today. While so-called experts told cofounder Alan Klapmeier that his new plane couldn't be built, or wouldn't obtain certification, or would fail to find a market, Klapmeier knew he had a winner. That's because, a pilot himself, he knew that the design and features of the plane fixed most of the problems that made flying difficult, dangerous, and expensive.

Fearless companies intuitively understand that all demons are illusions or, at least, are only matters of perception. Where others see risk or danger, these transformative companies see the most daunting pitfalls overshadowed by opportunity.

CHAPTER 4: PROCESS

Structure is freeing: That's the first of two lessons in this chapter. A company that can be very clear about what it does and what it doesn't do is a company for which choice comes easily. When corporate policies or product offerings are few and unambiguous, you don't accumulate needless hierarchy or eat up valuable time in decision-making exercises. Does this foreclose options for customers? Not necessarily. Chipotle Grill's limited menu simplifies the chain's management and quality control, for example, but it still leaves a hungry customer thousands of ways to combine ingredients and create a very satisfying meal.

Netflix offers a different inflection of the same idea, this time with people, where much of the company's human resources policy is a nonpolicy. The company has no set vacation policy and eschews ubiquitous expense limits and ethics standards in favor of a single admonition: "Act in Netflix's best interests." The DVD company believes it has sidestepped most structural impediments to growth simply by not establishing any such boundaries—and that brings us to the second and perhaps more important lesson of this chapter.

Transformative companies know that what they do or do not do with regard to process and how they hire and train new employees foretells their future growth. From their earliest days, the companies in this chapter have been built for scale. In this chapter we will take a look at process decisions made by Zappos, the online shoe retailer, IT outsourcing company Cognizant Technologies, and Jim Koch, founder of Boston Beer Company and Samuel Adams beer, who planned from the outset to create a national craft brewing market that could rival the Anheuser-Busches of the world. Koch made fundamental decisions with that goal in mind, even when his advisors might have thought he was reaching too far too soon.

CHAPTER 5: IRREVERENCE

An irreverent corporate culture can include crazy hats, jungle-theme cubicles, and a shared belief that wacky humor is essential to the job. Zappos, the online shoe retailer, is a prime example of the form. But irreverence is an elective condition that expresses itself in many ways, not all of them zany. The Southwest Airlines workforce feels empowered to do things differently, whether it's redesigning their tickets to suit their own needs, or not charging for baggage. It also can mean holding toilet-paper races on long flights, or reciting flight safety advisories in rap. At the opposite end of the spectrum, irreverence is also associated with Springfield Remanu-facturing (now known as SRC), a Missouri-based parts and service company whose CEO executed a successful turnaround by making it a company-wide game to hit the quarterly numbers, complete with tote boards and prizes. That now-famous CEO, Jack Stack, recognized that there was no need to assume that blue-collar workers with high school educations couldn't think like managers—or even CFOs.

Irreverence is anything a company does that doesn't pay obeisance to "The Way We've Always Done It." It's not rebellion; it's being willing to create the right space and conditions for bringing to life something transformative in a corporate setting. Could Zappos have become a customer-service powerhouse without doing something to lift the work beyond mere call-center drudgery? Could Southwest have made airline discounting work without being willing to color outside the lines? Could Jack Stack have taught his people how to save their own jobs without making a game of it?

Maybe, but probably not. These companies recognized that they required a certain creative density to succeed. They needed committed people who were willing to do things differently. They then worked to develop a corporate culture that attracted and retained legions of high-quality personnel.

CHAPTER 6: BANISHING SMALL THINKING

Thinking big is part of the romance of American capitalism, but, in reality, most corporations play it safe and think incrementally. In fact, the latest management fad is the Lean program, an *homage* to thinking small. In managing and choosing tactics to carry out strategy, most companies iterate and reiterate. Rarely do they step out of established patterns and make a bold move. This chapter celebrates the transformative companies that habitually accomplish the unexpected or supposedly ill-advised thing and find success. Along the way, we identify a few well-known corporations whose small thinking cost them huge opportunities.

There are a few basic conditions that must be present to allow a company to banish small thinking. The first is a culture that either outlaws devil's advocates or keeps them at bay. Maintaining that its company's culture and market position required special handling, Google was able to insist upon a raft of audacious particulars when it raised capital, including the right to pick its own traditionally recalcitrant venture capitalists and make them work together, without giving the group—or even Google's own CEO—much hope of influencing decisions. Intuit, meanwhile, banished small thinking when it repriced a product introduction as an impulse buy and removed copy protection to encourage word-of-mouth and achieve faster market penetration.

Companies that banish small thinking are, as Amazon founder Jeff Bezos says, "willing to be misunderstood." Many also take a longer-than-average view, waiting patiently for their approach to prove to be the right one. Finally, these tend to be companies that tolerate risk and failure well. Facebook, in fact, goes so far as to tell employees to "move fast and break things," knowing that getting a new app up quickly is worth the possibility of making a mistake. And when Netflix's in-house IT people continually failed to find a better algorithm for recommending movies to its customers, it took a deep breath and asked the world's nerds to come together and brainstorm the solution. The company offered—and delivered—a check for $1 million to the winners.

CHAPTER 7: APPETITE FOR DESTRUCTION

The companies mentioned in this chapter transform themselves by carrying out a lethal mission—to kill or radically alter an existing market, technology, or structure. They go where others have not thought to or have been unwilling to tread.

In this chapter we examine the likes of Amazon, Apple, *American Idol*, and Craigslist. Each changed or extirpated longstanding ways of delivering products and services, often toppling institutions, redesigning supply chains, and establishing themselves with the public as the heralds of an enhanced future. While Amazon, Apple, and *American Idol* were cold-blooded about their desire to topple the entertainment industry as we knew it, the effect that Craigslist had on newspapers was less intentional but just as devastating. In all cases, these companies and their founders held a torch to everything in their path. With confidence in their timing, methods, and technology, they marched forward to create the future.

CHAPTER 8: DETACHMENT

The ability to step outside ourselves and look dispassionately upon things as they are, rather than as we wish them to be, is hard won, especially in Western culture. We move too quickly. We make a religion out of going with our guts. We say we don't have time to think and make a joke of it.

However, transformative companies demonstrate a bias for inaction at regular intervals. They are what I call *proactively inactive* and they find ways to pause and course-correct. Bill Gates' Think Week is legendary, especially because it gave him the chance to see the opportunity he was missing on the Internet. Microsoft turned almost on a dime. Jeff Bezos of Amazon also makes it a practice to step away for a period of time almost quarterly.

Detachment and reflection need not be a CEO-only activity. Companies such as Google have allowed employees to spend up to one-fifth of their time on their own chosen projects, the result being new ideas for the corporation to pursue. Cognizant Technologies, the IT outsourcer, searches for inflection points that trigger a self-examination involving not only the company but also its customers. Other companies have created university-like environments where individual inquiry or research is expected.

Perhaps the newest entrant on the detachment and reflection front is a very old one—meditation. Companies are teaching meditation and offering employees the opportunity to clear their minds of the mundane chatter that prevents them from achieving an outsider's view of what's really going on.

CHAPTER 9: REINVENTION

Of all the chapters in this book, this one is the most traditionally Hindu. For corporations, reinvention is reincarnation.

Transformative companies are able to do business differently when crisis strikes or opportunity presents itself. Setting aside old policies, disassembling existing structures, even severing entire lines of business in favor of new ones—this is the hardest of hard work. What it takes to pull it off is the ability to value the needs of the market and its customers over those of the established corporate structure and, yes, even the people within it. This ability to pivot, more than anything else, is what it takes to be *built for change*.

Some companies reinvent themselves to keep a product or technology relevant, as has Hilti, the international tools manufacturer. Others have made it a part of their culture, as UPS has, in continually reinventing the services it offers to suit the shifting needs of its customers. Still others, such as computer maker Dell, have revamped not what they do, but how they do it. Responding to an outpouring of online vitriol against its customer service practices, Dell completely reinvented the function—and gave customers an uncensored voice with which to dialog with the company on customer service matters. Intuit, too, had to reinvent a structure for itself after it outgrew its entrepreneurial way of doing things.

The fact that these companies were successful in their reinvention is great, but it isn't the point. The point is that they understand the need to reinvent and habitually rally the will power to do it. That's what makes them transformative.

CHAPTER 10: BECOMING *BUILT FOR CHANGE*

Here we answer the key question: "How can my company become *built for change*?"

Through a series of open-ended and sometimes abstract questions that are intended to stimulate thought and internal debate, I hope to help you and your company—whether new or well-established—find the way toward a more transformative future.

Chapter 2

UNIVERSALITY

Shiva dances, surrounded by flames. Tradition has it that the blazing enclosure represents the cosmos, the whole perceived universe. Matter and energy swirl around the dancer, creating and destroying, always transforming. Just as the Shiva image encompasses the known and unknown world, businesses that tap into *universal themes connect with what's deep inside each one of us*, often striking the match that ignites a new paradigm.

It must have been confounding for Larry Page and Sergey Brin back in 1997. Every major Web portal in existence had taken a pass on the highbrow search technology that the pair had developed at Stanford University. Nobody was willing to pay even $1 million to license the technology. Developments in search technology were over, said the likes of Yahoo and Excite. The box was already on everybody's home page; what more did anybody need? Yet here was Google, eating up every spare byte at Stanford and bringing in 10,000 search queries a day. Obviously, this new search engine was gaining a following. So Brin and Page soldiered on. Maybe somebody would make something of their overgrown math project someday. If not, well, maybe they'd try making a company out of it themselves.

There are concepts that span continents, ideas that cross ideologies and connect with people's most elemental goals. As we know from Google's story, these connections often go unnoticed, at least at first. But when the light breaks through and new technology or a business concept reaches the universal, the results can be astounding. As the saying in the venture capital industry goes, it's like running downhill.

You can't confer wisdom, but you can sell the search for *knowledge*, which is Google's product.

You can't deliver love, but you can sell *connection*, like Facebook.

You can't promise upward mobility, but you can sell *empowerment* in unpredictable times, as LinkedIn does.

You may not be destined to become a retail titan, but you can *trade* like one when you buy and sell on eBay.

You can't sell peace or relaxation, but you can sell *escape*, as Starbucks seeks to do with each hot cup of designer coffee.

These companies are transformative by dint of their ability to connect effortlessly to basic human goals and desires: love, curiosity, significance, connectedness. And after the initial breakthrough it's this universality that attracts so much competition and emboldens multiple companies to attack the same markets. However, the ability to achieve and sustain a universal connection is harder than you might think. What's more, it's ephemeral; the ideas are constant but the best context in which to deliver them changes.

Clearly, some of the aforementioned companies were more transformative in the past than they are today, but that's the intriguing nature of universality. It isn't something you can protect like a trademark, and, therefore, it's difficult to claim as yours and yours alone for long. Competitors arise who are capable of closely mimicking the magic and addressing the same zeitgeist. Internal decisions are made that dilute the company's appeal with the public. Time passes and things change, but if there is a Holy Grail in business, it's that one idea that will address wants and needs that are universal. The companies in this early chapter of *Built for Change* have, however briefly or imperfectly, known it and lived it, and they have changed the world as a result.

Companies that succeed in channeling something universal to the marketplace are the ultimate in high-concept productions, with founding propositions that can be expressed not in a sentence but in a single word. And so elemental is that word, so impactful, that nothing more need be said. That's why transformative companies that have tapped into universality are not typically big advertisers or self-promoters, especially initially. Everybody gets it already, and word spreads virally. Everybody wonders why somebody hadn't thought of an enterprise like this sooner. Even when they do market, all external and, especially, internal communication reinforces the universal concepts within their business proposition.

Because it requires no explanation to anybody, a company that has universality going for it rarely strains to find customers—or, for that matter, employees. It's as though everyone in the company's orbit recognizes that there's something special going on. Moreover, except for those who pride themselves in not joining the herd, everybody wants to be part of it. Joining in extinguishes a collective catalepsy and makes one feel better, smarter, more fulfilled, more significant. Whatever this quality is, it's addictive, because the universality of the enterprise is strumming notes that are deep inside the customer and not easily accessed in other ways.

Of the eight transformational traits I've identified, universality may seem to be a strange place to start the discussion. Certainly it's the most ephemeral of the eight, but universality is no harder to figure out than the other characteristics that come later in the book, and it's just as vulnerable to the effects of time and neglect as any of the others. Just because we can't always fully prescribe universality doesn't mean we shouldn't describe it or strive for it. Indeed, understanding it will give us all a better sense of how to recognize universality in its nascent form. After all, wouldn't you like to be the person who owns the next Google for a million bucks?

What we see in companies that transform via their universality is a business that is intuitively based and understood and seemingly effortless in its execution. They're naturals, these companies. There's no strategic secret sauce; rather, the strategy is transparent, which is why competition is a given. Once accessed, the competitive dynamic becomes purely tactical, and superior execution becomes the sole differentiator.

Nor is there a user manual, because nothing going on in these enterprises needs explanation. When you see a Google search box, you know what to do. And what is it you do? You don't search for something, you "Google it." The company name is now a verb. In fact, "Google" was added to dictionaries in 2006 as a synonym for search, and it became the most popular word of the decade in 2009. If that isn't proof of universality, what is?

DIGITAL CONNECTION ON A GLOBAL SCALE

You don't have to have read Robert Putnam's *Bowling Alone* to conclude we are a lonely and disconnected culture. Nobody stays in one place, and, as a result, friendships and family ties languish. Less than a decade ago, it would have been unimaginable to reconnect with dozens of friends and acquaintances dating back to childhood in a matter of days, if not hours. Staying in constant touch with someone you met on a vacation or at a high school reunion? Until recently, you wouldn't have even let it cross your mind.

When Facebook came along, connection became possible—what its CEO calls an Elegant Organization—with everyone: family, friends, and friends of friends. Facebook welcomed 2010 with the story of a lost camera returned to its owner, thanks to Australian user Danny Cameron. He found the camera on the Greek isle of Mykonos and, through a group he established called Needle in a Haystack, Cameron mobilized 235,000 users to look at the camera's photos and send them to friends in the hope of finding the owner. Amazingly, the camera was returned to a French tourist just two weeks later. This is an extreme example of the power of connection—but it's one that Facebook founders think will soon become almost ordinary.

Like Google, Facebook was born on an elite college campus. The story is now familiar: Founder Mark Zuckerberg was a Harvard University student who, one fateful night, was looking for diversion from a love life gone sour. Hacking into dorm ID photos, the computer science major began tinkering with students' images, comparing them with animals. Then it became two students, in a sort of Harvard version of Hot or Not. Zuckerberg's little pastime generated 450 visitors and 22,000 photo views in its first four hours online. Harvard shut it down a few days later and charged Zuckerberg with a variety of offenses that were eventually dropped. But after Zuckerberg created comment-enabled pages for artworks under study in his art history class, the components that would become Facebook were in place. With Harvard eventually condoning it, Zuckerberg and some classmates created Facebook first for Harvard, then for all the Ivy League schools, then for campuses nationwide. Now, of course, it's open to anybody anywhere.

Along the way, Zuckerberg famously turned down a $1 billion buyout offer from Yahoo, saw his site gradually overtake predecessor MySpace, and watched as it became a social-networking juggernaut—especially on college campuses. In a 2006 study conducted by Student Monitor, a New Jersey-based company that specializes in knowing what college students care about, Facebook was ranked higher than the iPod—and deadlocked in a tie with beer.

Original aims notwithstanding, Zuckerberg has long maintained that the goal of his company is not so much profit as pluralism. Facebook's mission as stated on its Web site is "to give people the power to share and make the world more open and connected." Now that the site regularly plays a role in politics, crime-solving, entertainment, and everything in between, Facebook seems capable of anything its users can conceive of and implement. It already publishes more in a day than most other publications have in the whole of their existence. And, like Google, Facebook has managed to make an impact on language. The noun "Facebook" made it into the *Collins English Dictionary* in 2008. A year later, the *New Oxford American Dictionary* made "unfriend" its verb of the year.

What's universal about Facebook is, well, its universality. With a user base pushing 400 million worldwide, it's an all-comers site, a place accessible to high and low levels of economic and educational achievement alike, a place where the motley nature of a life's worth of connections is on full display. Sociologists love the site. In a *New York Times* article in late 2007 describing a burgeoning field of scientific research enabled by Facebook, journalist Stephanie Rosenbloom called the social networking site "a petri dish for the social sciences." And what makes Facebook such a sociological phenomenon? For one thing, it takes users back to an era where all towns were small towns and everybody knew everything about everyone else. With Facebook, the community may be worldwide, but it retains a human scale as people post the occurrences in their lives down to the smallest, most inane details. This offers the user what social scientists call "ambient awareness" of many lives. Researchers say this is something that humanity hasn't really achieved beyond the village compound before. Through the constant flow of tiny bits of mundane information on Facebook's once-controversial News Feed, one can assemble a surprisingly broad understanding of the people you've friended. It's been likened to a pointillist painting—many dots up close combining to provide a true picture at a distance.

Sociologists are plainly enjoying this huge, new data set. Facebook allows them to study how young people build social capital, which is a factor in most human interactions. Researchers also hope to use Facebook to determine something that's always been elusive—does taste determine friendship or does friendship determine taste? In other words, do birds of a feather really flock together?

CEO Zuckerberg leaves the sociology to the sociologists and instead focuses on the more prosaic goal of expanding market share. He has encouraged a thousand flowers to bloom by allowing users to develop applications and features for the site. He has shown reluctance to get involved in any policing of the site and the behavior of its users, though it has happened. At the same time, Zuckerberg has been perhaps surprisingly willing to fight user opinion, especially in matters, such as advertising, that affect Facebook's eventual profitability. He seems to know that he can do that, as long as he continues to offer users something they've never had before and can't find anywhere else—a continuing and intimate connection to other people in the world.

Zuckerberg is perhaps too taciturn to wax eloquent on the emotional importance of connection. But examples such as the returned camera speak loudly on his behalf. Said camera-finder Cameron when contacted for comment by the Facebook Blog: "My simple act found that it is possible to be a noncommercial, nondenominational person just performing a random act of kindness...I was happy to find [nearly] 250,000 other people who shared that philosophy. If the whole online community could be optimistic, full of hope and good will, then the possibilities for our capabilities would know no bounds."

EMPOWERING THE FREE AGENCY ECONOMY

Soon after Dan Nye became CEO of LinkedIn, the online professional network, engineers showed him a cool tool they had put together. It was a static representation of the world that had a plethora of green lines shooting from place to place, even continent to continent, as LinkedIn members connected with one another in real time. Insiders found it an exhilarating, dazzling fireworks show. Outsiders, however, were less impressed.

It was 2007, at the height of Facebook's growth. Adults had discovered the college-born social-networking site and began signing up in droves. Nye found himself sitting across the desk from more than one reporter who wanted him to justify LinkedIn's continued existence. How could it compete against Facebook, especially now that the social networking site had made itself an open platform like Windows?

Nye acknowledged the threat. But it wasn't long before he was able to convince people—including himself—that LinkedIn would be fine despite Facebook's growth. The reporters who were proudly telling him how they were using Facebook to chase leads weren't expanding their network by searching for particular skills or industry affiliations; you can't do that on Facebook. They were simply calling up names they already knew and messaging them to seek sources for stories. If they used LinkedIn instead, they could be finding sources they don't already know and seeking advice from a network that had more than 20 million people at that time. On LinkedIn, the people in the network would likely compete to provide the best answer, knowing that a high quality answer or "best answer" would be a nice addition to the professional profile they maintain on LinkedIn.

During the same timeframe, Nye gave a speech in which he did a bit of show-and-tell. First, he called up his LinkedIn profile which showed professional content that he controlled, then he opened Facebook, where someone had posted a video of a bulldog riding a skateboard. "Think about the difference," he told me, recalling the contrast he drew that day. "LinkedIn is all about presenting yourself professionally whereas Facebook is all about communication and entertainment." The message is clear and profound: you don't need to abjure your professional image to connect instantaneously on a global scale.

The truth was plain to see: Facebook offers connection, but LinkedIn offers something more sophisticated yet equally aspirational: *empowerment*. And that's what makes LinkedIn a transformative company in the category of universality—the way in which it empowers its users to build and maintain a career-enhancing profile, find people and opportunities, collaborate with these people, gather data, share files, and solve problems.

Despite having left LinkedIn in 2009, Nye remains one of its biggest fans. He believes that the site meets a need that has only become more critical with each passing year—the desire to take command of one's own career. In a recent conversation he told me, "We live in the free agent economy now. Companies have no problem downsizing; they add and shed jobs at will. Whether it's a big company or a small one, there is no such thing anymore as lifetime employment. People need to be empowered to take their career—and the way it's presented—into their own hands, making sure they are happy and advancing where they are, that they're making enough money and living where they want to. If not, LinkedIn empowers you to fulfill your potential on your own."

LinkedIn's success stories are many. Companies use it to scout out potential acquisitions and reference-check prospective employees. Executive recruiters use it to bring clients a wider and better-qualified pool of applicants. However, the core of the network is made up of the multitudes of individuals who use it to seek advice from a former business contact, to highlight recent accomplishments that might bring a job inquiry, or to find just the right person for a position that has recently opened. In fact, Nye himself checked references on key LinkedIn personnel before taking the CEO position. Then, after he took the job, he started using the network to hire subordinates. For example, he wanted to find a Silicon Valley–based vice president with experience at a large consumer products company who had also worked at an Internet startup. "In five minutes an employee sent me eight people who fit the profile, all of them within 30 minutes of Mountain View," Nye told me. "I reference-checked them and managed to talk to each of them on the phone within days. And I thought to myself, wow, this is a powerful tool."

The tagline at LinkedIn is "relationships matter," because that's where the empowerment lies. It's not just who you know; it's how they know you *and* who they know. As Nye explained it to me, "LinkedIn helps you leverage your network and the networks of *contacts* to expand your assets and capabilities. It helps you to be more successful across a forty-year career." Nye says, "your professional network is something you carry with you until the day you retire."

REDUCING THE TRADE DEFICIT

There is a reason why *The Price Is Right* was a huge daytime TV hit, and it's also why PBS has an unexpected winner with *Antiques Road Show.* Most humans love a bargain, like to test their abilities in estimating the value of something in the marketplace, or seek appreciation in the value of something they own. Yet, until fairly recently, it was only a spectator sport—not many average Americans directly participated in setting prices, bargaining, bidding, or negotiating. This has changed as the Internet has matured, and eBay has led the way. Like little else, eBay has tapped into the universal desire to wheel and deal, to *trade* in a marketplace much larger than the neighborhood garage sale or the local newspaper's classified section. That's eBay's brand of universality.

The affinity some users feel for eBay borders on the irrational, so it's perhaps not surprising that the buying and selling behavior on the site can be similarly unpredictable. Many a scholarly paper and popular blog post has been written about eBay pricing patterns, describing how people will pay more to avoid a high shipping cost—even when the math of the total cost argues against it. They have also documented how a low starting bid stimulates auction bidding, resulting in a higher sales price. Nevertheless, for many eBay users, none of this is a deterrent to participation or even merits a change in behavior. At the beginning of this chapter, I spoke of the addictive quality seen in companies that are transformative via universality; and eBay is a strong example of that attribute. Indeed, eBay claims that its first sale was a broken laser pointer for $14.83, and the lore of that first sale has migrated from corporate histories to publications that include the *Telegraph* of London. It's said that when founder Pierre Omidyar followed up with the buyer to ensure he knew the item was broken, he was told, "I'm a collector of broken laser pointers."

eBay has encouraged the native trading instinct that lives inside many of its patrons by exerting little or no control over what occurs on the site. It's the market that sets the price, the market that rates sellers for reliability, and the market—with only rare instances of intervention—that determines what's too controversial to be sold. "I wanted to give the power of the market back to individuals," founder Pierre Omidyar told *Business Week* back in 2004. (He also admits that part of his motivation in starting the business was to provide his wife with a place to buy and sell the Pez dispensers she collected.)

Of course, in its early days there were plenty of disbelievers—people who strongly doubted that people would pay someone they'd never met to ship them something they'd never seen. But the eBay phenomenon, like many companies that connect with the universal, has had an appeal that defies logic or predictors of typical behavior. Studies and statistics quantify Omidyar's success: Today eBay operates in 30 countries worldwide and claims to have hundreds of millions of users. The U.S. Census Bureau says eBay and similar online storefronts have caused a bump in the number of Americans who opt to go into business for themselves. Indeed, between 2003 and 2004, a period of high growth for eBay, the number of self-employed Americans grew by 1 million, to 19.5 million. While it represents an increase of less than 5 percent, the boom becomes more apparent when you narrow the field to include just electronic shopping and mail-order businesses run by sole proprietors. The increase then jumps to 12.7 percent for the period.

eBay has not only recognized its role in stimulating entrepreneurship; it has also embraced it. The company has held annual community conferences that feature motivational business speakers and entrepreneurial skill-building classes. eBay doesn't shy away from claiming its universality, either. The theme of one conference, for example, was "The Power of All of Us."

THE GREAT ESCAPE

In all the tomes that have been written about Starbucks, there is one aspect that gets relatively little notice. It's the company's third-place concept. Yes, there are early articles and some more recent retrospectives that speak of founder Howard Schultz's desire to create a third place—not home, not work, but someplace else for people to congregate. But it's surprising to me how many scribes and commentators discard the idea after a paragraph. Some even disregard it with a bit of sarcasm, as if it were a nostrum prescribed by some New Age guru: *Create the third place.*

To me, the third-place concept cannot be dissociated from the company's extraordinary impact; indeed, it's at the core of all that Starbucks has achieved. It's what makes the company transformative and has spurred thousands of imitators worldwide. In this case, the one-word concept that reaches inside customers and hooks them is *escape*. Your average Starbucks is a cozy place where the seats are well-cushioned, the music is good, and you can get Wi-Fi on your laptop. It's busy, too, and that's key. People love to be where other people are—especially if they have the feeling they've left the world behind.

Customers know nothing of the third place per se. It's actually a term coined by the urban sociologist Ray Oldenburg when writing about the importance of gathering places. The term was then adopted by Starbucks' founder, Howard Schultz, to try to explain why European coffeehouses—his model for Starbucks—are so central to society in places like Milan. Escape is the universal word for what makes Starbucks relatable, and I was pleased to find that it resonates with Stanley Hainsworth, the man most responsible for developing and implementing the third-place concept for Starbucks.

Stanley is a soft-spoken Southerner who came to Starbucks after being an actor and the creative director for both Nike in the United States and Lego in Denmark. At Starbucks, Hainsworth connected with the third-place concept and remains hooked still.

In a conversation I had with him, I asked: "What creates the third place? How did Starbucks manage to convey the idea of escape without ever actually saying it?" His reply: "If you look at Starbucks, making great coffee is the price of entry. It has to be good if people are going to want to sip it in a chair. So it's coffee first, and everything else is an adjacency—pastries, books, music, chocolate, whatever. The third place is the differentiator. You can get good coffee and these other things elsewhere, but Starbucks created the environment with the great coffee and made it a hangout and a place to get away even for a few minutes."

"The secret," Hainsworth continues, "is that everything matters, everything you do. It's the furniture, the artwork, the color of the walls, the things you display on the shelf, the packaging, the way they fulfill the order and hand it to you, the music—it all adds up to a whole."

At Starbucks, Hainsworth created a five-layer filter for each element that was being considered for inclusion in any Starbucks location, from signage to cups to napkins. Was it: *handcrafted, artistic, human, sophisticated, and enduring?* "The words all have to work together," Hainsworth told me. "You look for things that speak to the human condition, the soul, things that touch you in some way—copy that talks the way a human speaks, for example." According to Hainsworth, it was often easier to consider the five filters as a group rather than individually. "Sophisticated was always the especially hard one, though it was easier to define alongside the others."

Still, even as we reverse engineer the design concept, it remains difficult to describe why the third-place concept actually worked. Hainsworth himself isn't sure. "It exceeded anyone's expectations of where it could go," he says. "It created a global sensation." Right time, right concept, he supposes.

I asked Hainsworth to describe the value proposition of the third place. What, really, is the customer being offered? His thoughts went back to when he himself had worn the green apron, because, like most Starbucks employees, Hainsworth put in several one-week stints as an in-store worker. What sticks with him even years later, in his new pursuits, is the personal interactions between customers and baristas, and the ebb and flow of customer traffic throughout the day, each part of the day having its own clientele and character. More than anything, the essential element to creating escape seemed to be a feeling of community.

"It's an amazing place," Hainsworth explains. "You walk into a store and you see groups of people—a homeowners' association meeting in the corner, a father and a kid working on homework together, couples hanging out—it's a slice of the community. That's why small towns and suburban areas were always especially excited to get a Starbucks—it met a need for a gathering place."

Hainsworth recalls how teens would seem to be on their best behavior when at a Starbucks, and how adults would acknowledge one another as if they were guests in the same living room. He suspects these responses reflect a certain gratitude for the experience offered—yes, the escape of it.

Hainsworth explains, "We can call you by name, make the best drink we can for you, maybe make you feel better about yourself and humanity for a moment."

Unfortunately, Starbucks has learned of late how fleeting universality can be. By its own success, Starbucks has single-handedly energized an entire coffeehouse sector of the economy—making the company not only a great example of universality but also, perhaps, a victim of its own achievements. Countless arrivistes can simulate the Starbucks experience closely enough to bleed off customers and reduce some of the cachet. Meanwhile, Starbucks' decision to sell packets of instant coffee may be diluting its brand promise.

The chords strummed by a universal company are deep ones, and though they may eventually fade away, they resonate long. Indeed, somehow the companies in this chapter have managed to sync their business with human aspirations and goals. Their timing is spot-on. Their products and services seem to be just what people have been looking for—without their even knowing it. To the great envy of unsuccessful entrepreneurs everywhere, the world greets these enterprises with open arms.

Chapter 3

FEARLESSNESS

Faced with anger, confusion, or chaos, we instinctively raise an outward-facing palm of the hand that says, "Slow down. I am calm, so you be calm." Shiva's upraised hand, a symbolic gesture known as the *abhaya mudra*, represents protection, peace, and the dispelling of doubt. Transformative companies are *fearless*. They understand that all demons are illusions of our own making. Where others see risk or danger, transformative companies see opportunity.

When Michael Chasen surveyed the landscape of educational technology in the mid-1990s, he saw signposts pointing to a revolutionary future. He noted a huge spike in demand for student access to the Internet on college campuses. Where it wasn't being provided to them, students were actually voting with their feet and refusing to enroll—that's how much they wanted a wired dorm room. Seemingly overnight, it had become imperative that schools and universities scramble to invest millions in wiring their campuses. Yet there remained one gaping omission: there was no software being added to the hardware. Little or nothing was being done to leverage the new communications infrastructure for improved learning. Professors were still tracking assignments in grade books, and students were still straining their necks and squinting their eyes to see grades posted on hallway walls.

That's where Chasen and his founding partner, Matthew Pittinsky, saw opportunity. They quit their junior consulting jobs at KPMG Peat Marwick—posts that had had them working on information technology projects for a variety of schools, universities, and the federal Department of Education—and in 1997 they started Blackboard, the now-$300-plus million company that is the leading portal for services to educators, students, and educational institutions worldwide. The company employs more than 1,000 people and serves more than 5,000 educational institutions in 60 countries. Even at its relatively young age, Blackboard is creating a legacy in information technology. A half-dozen or more companies have been spun out of Blackboard by former employees.

Blackboard now has an air of inevitability about it, with many on the sidelines no doubt wondering why they hadn't been the ones to think of this obvious play. However, Blackboard encountered its share of doubters in the early years, Chasen told me recently. Not only were there competitors already in the space, the rap was that they were plagued by reluctant customers and end users. "When we started trying to raise our initial capital, our investor called about a dozen schools and they all said, no, they wouldn't buy Blackboard, because teachers wouldn't use it," Chasen recalls. "These institutions thought their professors were Luddites who wouldn't know how to use the new technology and wouldn't want to learn how."

To Chasen and Pittinsky, the reaction was stupefying. As they saw it, the signposts of impending change in educational technology were klieg-lit and all but flashing in an attempt to gain the business world's attention. Yet almost nobody was acting, and true believers were hard to find. Chasen couldn't see how they could be missing the signs that were *right there*. So obvious were they—to him and Pittinsky, anyway—that people almost had to choose willfully not to see them, like the nakedness of the main character in "The Emperor's New Clothes."

Today, thanks to Blackboard, it is commonplace for teachers to post syllabi online, to make and receive assignments, to moderate discussions, to track student progress, and to provide linked access to a variety of learning resources. Indeed, the Motley Fool site's bloggers have joked that Blackboard has put an end to the slacker's excuses for not getting academic work done. They mourn, "The days when classes merely passed the time between parties? Gone." No longer can students claim they were sick and missed the assignment, or couldn't find the reading list, or any of the other time-honored slacker excuses. It's all on Blackboard. In fact, Blackboard is rapidly becoming the way most things get done on campus. Blackboard also disseminates campus emergency information, assists schools with collecting payments of various kinds, and is further expanding its repertoire with the inclusion of iPhone apps. Even the final frontier has been penetrated: where once educators scoffed at the idea of conducting tests online, it's widely accepted now—and Chasen says even college-entrance exams could be administered via Blackboard, if the college board so chose.

"People really underestimated the rate at which teachers would adopt the technology," Chasen told me. Not that Chasen considers the change to have been particularly rapid; in fact, after more than a decade in business, Chasen thinks Blackboard has only recently reached a tipping point in its huge market. But he never envisioned anything but steady and inevitable adoption: "High school kids become college students who become teachers—creating a new generation that is very familiar with and expecting technology." Today the questions greeting admissions officers tend to include IT issues. "Prospective students ask, 'What does your technological infrastructure look like?' and 'Can I get my course materials online?' The answers help them make their choice of where to go to school."

Niccolo Machiavelli once said, "There is nothing more difficult to take in hand, more perilous to conduct, or more uncertain in its success, than to take the lead in the introduction of a new order of things." Blackboard qualifies as a transformative company because its story displays a distinct type of fearlessness—the kind that persists in the face of all that Machiavelli describes.

But what others see as fearlessness feels like something quite different to the entrepreneurs themselves. Having combined my venture capital experience with some research, I've come to believe that this difference in perception is the secret ingredient in their ability to transform.

For Michael Chasen, there really was no vacillating once he'd seen a new educational technology market in front of him and ripe for the plucking. Certainly he had some concerns about exactly how Blackboard would address this market opportunity. (Chasen chose a subscription model over the ad-based approach his competitors favored and was proven right in the dot.com bust.) However, there was never any doubt in the young CEO's mind that the market would develop into something very robust.

Indeed, the concept of risk almost did not enter Chasen's mind. In our interview we discussed this risk-blindness, noting that for some people a particular market may seem risky, but for the more transformative business, it seems almost more risky not to do it than to do it. That clicked with Chasen. He replied, "That is exactly it. Competitors didn't look at it that way, but we did, and that's what catapulted us ahead."

What prompted him to move forward? "We felt confident of the need for our software. We knew the value was significant. We almost had to do it."

"We almost had to do it." That, for me, is the key statement. Fearlessness may look to most of us like entrepreneurs allowing themselves to be pushed into a market, cavalierly discounting perilous risk. For transformative companies, however, the impulse derives from an undeniable, irresistible, inevitable personal conviction. They climb that mountain because to them it looks like Kansas prairie instead of Everest.

Interestingly, it is only in this context that Chasen accepts any sort of badge for entrepreneurial courage. "I guess it was rather bold of us to think we could change an industry that hadn't changed since Socrates." But that's an insight he didn't have when going up the mountain. It's the kind you gain when you look back to see where you've been.

GENERAL AVIATION'S FEAR OF FLYING

Alan Klapmeier, cofounder of Cirrus Designs, an aircraft manufacturing company based in Duluth, Minnesota, is another transformative entrepreneur who wants to fine-tune our understanding of risk. When he and I talked in late 2009, he was seeking funding for a second airplane startup, having left Cirrus to his brother, Dale, and a team of successor-managers. Klapmeier really warmed to the topic of fearlessness or risk-blindness, and I found him eager to share his perspective on the motivations that undergird transformative entrepreneurship. If I had to summarize his point of view, it's perhaps that knowledge is power. He thinks the market has, to its detriment, stopped believing that a guy can actually know what he's doing. Fearlessness, he says, is just the word we project on people who act on what they know.

Cirrus came into the world saying it would build an affordable, piston-engine, four-seater airplane that would be joystick-navigable, cheaper to fly (thanks to new, lightweight materials), and both easier and more comfortable to fly (owing to better pilot visibility and a computer screen primary flight display that provides a complex set of information at a glance). More importantly, the Cirrus aircraft would be safer, with fixed wheels that can never be anywhere but where they should be on landing. But the key and unique safety element was the inclusion of an airframe parachute designed to provide a troubled airplane with a softer landing.

Klapmeier's deep customer insight was hard-won; he had survived a mid-air collision in the 1980s that killed the other pilot. He saw improved survivability as the key factor in getting family members to sign off on anyone's decision to become a pilot and buy a plane. In other words, including the parachute was a bid toward reinvigorating the general aviation market.

Think of how this sounded in 1993 or so, when plans were still on the drawing board. Surely any of us would have considered it bold, fearless, and risk-denying to say you're going to build a new kind of privately owned aircraft, a modern answer to the Cessna. If it were possible to do everything Klapmeier wanted to do, wouldn't Cessna have done it already?

Klapmeier groans at the thought, having heard it far too many times in the early years of his company. He challenges: *Since when do we judge what's possible in a market by what the current leader is doing?* In fact, in Klapmeier's hit parade of stupid things said to him by would-be investors, that one is only exceeded by the guy who explained his firm's decision not to invest in Cirrus by saying: "I talked to one of my friends who's a pilot and he says private aviation is dead." A paroxysm of frustration engulfs Klapmeier at the memory. "You talked to a *friend*? That's what you call due diligence?"

Klapmeier can't fathom why people couldn't see what he was seeing—or, failing that, at least put a little faith in his vision. He *knew* that the Cirrus SR20 could be built, he *knew* it would sell, and with an improved plane on the market, he *knew* that private aviation would prove to be anything but dead. "Does the existence of the Internet mean that nobody is going to travel anymore, nobody's going to want to have an actual business meeting instead of a teleconference, or nobody's going to want to go see their grandchildren anymore?"

Klapmeier knew things that were even harder to believe. He knew—contrary to all the naysayers—that he could get the Federal Aviation Administration to certify a new type of privately owned airplane after having not done so for over 10 years. Even as would-be investors argued that he'd never maintain enough operating capital to cover the slow assembly of one plane at a time, Klapmeier knew he'd stay in business—aided by a plan to make buyers pay hefty and nonrefundable deposits that went straight into the company's general fund. The obvious question for us as observers is: How could he be so certain of all he supposedly knew?

Klapmeier credits two things: One was growing up in an entrepreneurial family where dinner conversation included profit and loss statements, cash flow, and questions as to what sort of businesses the kids were going to start someday. The other was Klapmeier's long and deep familiarity with aviation, which began almost before he could walk.

Alan Klapmeier was among the fussiest of babies. For the first two years of his life he cried anytime his mother wasn't maintaining eye contact with him. To gain a little peace, she found she could take him to a local airport to watch planes take off. Planes grew to be young Alan's passion. By high school he was flying on his own and telling friends he was going to build airplanes after college. He credits his liberal arts degree with teaching him how to think, question, criticize, and evaluate ideas—including business ideas.

The Klapmeier brothers first went into kit airplanes, marketing a composite pusher-engine craft called the VK30 beginning in 1984. It was big (four to five passengers), cigar-shaped, and the first kit plane to be featured on the cover of *Aviation Week and Space Technology*. But the enterprise, while successful, only whetted the brothers' appetites for greater things. When plans were laid for the manufacture of the certified plane, the SR20, the pair bought back all those kit planes. "In aviation your reputation is everything," Klapmeier explained during our interview. "Instead of declaring bankruptcy or going out of business and starting up again with a new name, we opted to put a box around the risk." After seeing one kit owner cut numerous holes in the fuselage to lighten the craft, and others installing ridiculously large engines, the buyback seemed a good way of heading off bad press.

The first certified plane, the SR20, came onto the market in 1999 after almost a decade of planning, fundraising, and testing. With its younger cousins the SR22 and the Turbo, the series is now the most popular aircraft in general aviation worldwide, with approximately 5,000 units in service. But even as the first SR20s were creating a sensation—as any new plane would in a market where "new" had come to mean 20 years old—the Klapmeier brothers were onto even greater things. Cirrus Designs has been working for several years on developing Vision, a personal jet.

In our discussion of risk, Klapmeier launched a fusillade at my chosen vocation, particularly on the topic of differentiating between real versus perceived risk. He asserts: "What the typical person in the financial world thinks of as risk is often not the real risk. They think, 'This person must be fearless, don't they know it can't be done?' But they don't know what they're talking about. They drive their cars by looking in the rear view mirror."

Risk, to Klapmeier, is starting a software company—or anything else that a lot of people are already doing admirably. He chose aviation precisely because nobody was doing much that was new there, where unique customer insights were rare, and his years of thinking about airplanes had shown him the opportunities that existed. He told me "You've got to be really fearless to say, 'I'm going to be the next Microsoft.' Being the next big aviation company wasn't nearly as much risk. But of course it's not seen that way in the financial industry."

Klapmeier's experiences had convinced him that, even if the customer didn't know it yet, there were enhancements to be made to small planes that would make all the difference in who flew planes and how often. "It's like Windows," he says. "There wasn't anything the computer could do the day after Windows that it couldn't do before. But it was easier, and easier changed everything."

Take, for example, Cirrus's revolutionary primary flight display (PFD). Klapmeier says a six-figure consultant's report maintained that customers didn't care if they moved from dials and gauges to a flat-screen display in landscape. "It was just wrong!" Klapmeier says. "You can't ask somebody who doesn't understand what the product is whether or not they'll value it. I told my board, 'I guarantee you they will value it and I guarantee that they won't know that until they try it.'" Klapmeier felt he knew what he was talking about, because he professes to be a "lousy" instrument pilot. "I didn't get a lot of utility out of an airplane because I knew I wasn't safe. I knew the PFD would change that." It has, for him and for many others. But it wouldn't have seen the light of day if Klapmeier hadn't stood up to the board and its consultant and insisted that PFD development continue. We call that fearless; Klapmeier considers it just plain truth telling.

Call it stubbornness, call it blind luck, or call it good timing, but Klapmeier's father had a saying about entrepreneurialism: You have to be dumb enough to start and smart enough to finish. However you choose to label it, the results are undeniable.

THE TENDERFOOT AT THE
STOCK EXCHANGE

No enterprise succeeds without being well-timed. Often, what appears fearless to the rest of us is actually an entrepreneur's hyper-awareness of a shift in his or her market—something imperceptible to many but dead obvious to the transformative entrepreneurs who spot the signals. Proximity to and familiarity with the domain is a help, as Chasen and Klapmeier have shown us, but what separates the folks who spot a new trend from those who know how to act on it is typically more than being close to the action. It takes a certain insight not only into what customers are clamoring for but also what they might embrace—if only it existed. That's how Blackboard's software has become a multifaceted portal that extends far beyond teacher-student communication. That's how Cirrus revitalized private aviation, by showing would-be customers that flying a plane could be as easy as—and not much more expensive than—driving a BMW.

A third example of transformative fearlessness can be found in the story of how a tiny brokerage metamorphosed into the Charles R. Schwab financial services empire. It's a tale in which both timing and customer intimacy play significant roles.

In 1975 Chuck Schwab was a typical investment advisor/stockbroker. He had a modest-sized clientele in California, built in part on a free Brownie camera for each new account. He would probably have remained in that business for the length of his career had not a Securities Exchange Commission decree set in motion a series of decisions that led to transformation.

The change was momentous. Commissions on financial transactions were deregulated. Many major firms took the opportunity to hike their rates, but others went the other direction and became discounters—Schwab among them. However, Schwab took a longer and broader view of what deregulation could mean. He foresaw a financial industry free of gatekeepers, dubiously valued advice in the form of internally generated research, cold calls, and hard sells. Instead, Joe Average could do his own research, assisted by a wealth of Schwab-provided resources, and thereby manage his own portfolio. To make the job as easy as possible, Schwab envisioned a 24-hour business day for these motivated investors, aided by toll-free telephone numbers, fax machines, and, eventually, the Internet. As all of this came about, the company adopted an invigorating purpose statement: "Helping everyone to become financially fit."

The key differentiator that Schwab offered small-time investors was no commissions. Instead of participating in the rate cutting that was happening throughout the discount end of the industry, he simply abolished the commissions and put everybody on salary. Then he blitzed the market, opening as many as 17 regional offices in a single year and heavily advertising the Schwab difference on national television. Within a decade, Schwab could boast 1 million customers and 20 percent of the discount business—which, in turn, represented 20 percent of the entire trading market.

Schwab's shot across the bow of the existing financial services industry came late but strong when, in 1984, he authored a book titled *How to Be Your Own Stockbroker*. In it, he painted brokers as self-interested and untrustworthy, the major investment firms as greedy, and the New York Stock Exchange as "ossified." Plenty of people on Wall Street today would find that description humorous, because the Charles R. Schwab business model now looks much more like the traditional brokerages it originally scorned. The "Talk to Chuck" ad campaign, for example, clearly offers not just information but advice. Once-rock-bottom fees are higher too, to compensate for revenues lost to Web trading.

But the history is what matters here, and just because the company appears anything but transformative today doesn't mean Schwab isn't fully deserving of the label. In fact, it's clear that Schwab was the one man, and his the one company, that made the stock market accessible to everyone. Schwab was the first to establish a computerized system to handle client transactions and record keeping. He was also the first to create a one-source group of no-load mutual funds, allowing businesses and their employees to move 401K money among them at will. Chuck Schwab also welcomed independent financial advisers, allowing anyone with the proper credentials to use Schwab's name, resources, and back-office services without having to become an employee. It spurred growth even further.

Yet Schwab's biggest contribution was his then-rare willingness to believe in the little guy. Just as Alan Klapmeier deplores the disdain with which aviation has traditionally regarded nonpilots, Schwab believed that individual investors were more capable of handling their own portfolios than Wall Street would have had them think. Echoing the universality theme of empowerment we illustrated through LinkedIn, we can see that Schwab was a financial populist. Where most feared the chaos of individual brokerage account management, Schwab knew differently. He had an unwavering belief from his own experience as a stockbroker that there was a cadre of small investors who were champing at the bit for the chance to control their own financial destiny. In its heyday, Schwab provided its customers with everything they needed, but never more than they wanted. This way, Chuck Schwab transformed an industry and left competitors scrambling to catch up with him.

THE CUSTOMER OBSESSION

As we've seen in our examples, one important element in the apparent fearlessness we see in transformative companies is a deep understanding of—if not total identification with—the customer. It's to the point of obsession: How can I make this person's life better, easier, more fulfilling? How can I make the customer's experience less of a hassle? Most importantly, how can I reinvigorate markets and enrich human activities by creating new opportunities?

When Chasen and Pittinsky founded Blackboard, they were only a few years past their fraternity years at American University. The needs of both students and professors were still very much in mind for them. When Alan Klápmeier and his brother founded Cirrus, it stemmed from pilot-centered knowledge of what gets people into the air in their own planes and keeps them flying, combined with all that they understood about what had yet to be provided to pilots in the way of flight-experience enhancements. For Charles Schwab, it was the almost revolutionary idea that the average Joe or Josephine not only could make his or her own investment decisions, but that he or she would want to. At some level, each of these companies and their entrepreneurs eschewed the normal ways in which customers are written off by established businesses—buyers are not interested, not smart enough, not ready for something new, and so on.

Amazon offers us some things to consider in this chapter, as it does in several places in this book. Whenever someone asks founder Jeff Bezos why he does what he does, why he engages Amazon in so many apparently disparate activities, often with long waits for payoff, he always attributes his moves to enhancing the customer experience. As observers we see what he does and conclude he must be fearless (or, in some eyes and instances, nuts). However, he at least *thinks* he's just moving the ball forward for his customer.

The Kindle reader, for example, is something that Bezos regards as perhaps the last step in making customer access to books and all printed material absolutely seamless. With a Kindle, you don't need a phone or a computer or a library card to read the book you're interested in. You order it up on the same device you will use to read it. This seamlessness is a goal that Bezos says has been uppermost in his mind for the past two decades that Amazon has been in business.

Still, critics complained when he embarked on the Kindle project, saying he was improvidently ignoring proven customer balkiness. Hadn't the market largely rejected the Sony Reader? But Bezos—not unlike Chasen and Klapmeier—was convinced that the market was only sluggish because it hadn't seen the right product. So Bezos and his team made key enhancements: obviation of the need to attach the device to the computer to download books, as was necessary with the Sony Reader, and the introduction of a new type of display that better mimics the look of print on a page. Clearly, the market has approved.

With his determination to develop the Kindle, Bezos was violating a cardinal rule that was most colorfully labeled by Tom Peters as "sticking to the knitting," and later described as core competency. Critics said that companies shouldn't be trying to do things they don't know how to do. By plunging forward, Bezos was exhibiting his fearlessness, but in ways different from Chasen, Klapmeier, or Schwab. The three latter transformational entrepreneurs were able to be fearless because they knew their domain so thoroughly, their knowledge having been born of prolonged, close contact with the players in the market. They almost granularly understood the wants and needs of their customers and the opportunities being presented in the marketplace.

Not necessarily so for Jeff Bezos: He has the confidence—some of it based on his vast resources, of course—to make judgments on factors other than what the company already knows how to do. And that makes him perhaps a different shade of fearless.

"Companies tend to get skills-focused, instead of customer-needs focused," Bezos told *Business Week* interviewer Peter Burrows in 2008. "When [companies] think about extending their business into some new area, the first question is, 'Why should we do that? We don't have any skills in that area.' That approach puts a finite lifetime on a company, because the world changes and what used to be cutting-edge skills will turn into something your customers may not need anymore. A much more stable strategy is to start with, 'What do my customers need?' and then do an inventory of the gaps in your skills. Kindle is a great example. If we [had] set our strategy by what our skills happen[ed] to be rather than by what our customers need[ed], we never would have done it. We had to go out and hire people who [knew] how to build hardware devices and create a whole new competency for the company."

Improving the customer's experience doesn't come cheaply or quickly. Almost always, the payback on Amazon's investments is slower than Wall Street would like and more corrosive to profit margins than investors appreciate. However, criticism doesn't faze Bezos. In an interview with Andrew Davidson of the *Sunday Times* of London, he said, "Look, every time we do something new we get criticized. The corollary is you rarely get criticized for acts of omission, yet the biggest mistakes companies make are what they should have done and failed to do."

Most corporate acts of omission are fully vetted, of course. Many a company today takes pride in having considered the existing market-place, benchmarked themselves against the competition and pronounced themselves ahead of the curve. They are competitive in their core competencies and therefore safe. But this says nothing of what consumers might want from a market's players or may be receptive to. Bezos is a high-profile example of somebody who's not willing to run his business by looking sideways or behind, as he made clear in a *Fortune* article in 2008. "Whatever your set of competitors is [doing] today is transitory," he reasoned. Pay attention to their moves and "you'd have to change your strategy all the time!" To those who struggle to comprehend Amazon's moves, Bezos offers insouciance, "We are very comfortable being misunderstood," he laughingly told Davidson in the 2007 *Sunday Times* interview. "That's [our] core competence."

We might also note, with Bezos's help, that patience is a necessary ingredient in fearlessness. After all, Chasen, Klapmeier, and Schwab built companies that were 10-year overnight successes. It's similar for Amazon. The company's story is full of plot points at which Bezos got ahead of the market or was forced to wait for technology and other factors to converge in his favor. "We are willing to plant seeds that take time to grow," he told the *New York Times'* Brad Stone, soon after Amazon began providing fulfillment services for other companies, a move many considered slow at best in bearing financial fruit. As Bezos described it in that case and others, it's of no particular concern to him or anyone else at Amazon when the payoff occurs, as long as it does.

"Our motto is *gradatim ferociter*," Bezos declaimed to talk show host Charlie Rose. "It means 'step by step ferociously.'" In the *Sunday Times* interview conducted in the same timeframe, Bezospoke of his delight in "exploring dark alleys that occasionally broaden into a wide vista." To walk that dark alley you must know more about your customers than perhaps they themselves do. As the fearless Henry Ford once remarked, "If I'd asked my customers what they wanted, they would have said a faster horse."

Chapter 4

PROCESS

Shiva's right hand holds an hourglass-shaped drum called a *damaru*. For business, the beating drum represents the sound and *process* of creative energy. It suggests a dynamic commitment to structure, control, and efficiency. Things may be unplanned, but they are seldom out of place or accidental. There is simplicity here, too. Process, like a drum, provides the backbeat for transformative businesses.

In the old TV spot, it's morning at the pier. A salty fisherman furtively eyes a stranger in full colonial garb. "I'm waiting for Sam Adams' noble hops. They should be here any minute!" says the man in breeches and buckled shoes. He begins penning "welcome" on a signboard, and while he does, he explains that Sam Adams beer uses only the finest Bavarian noble hops. "Would you like to do the Bavarian hops dance with me?" he asks. "It goes like this." While the patriot prances and preens, a distant ship's horn sounds the arrival of the shipment. "They're here!" he exults.

When Jim Koch founded Boston Brewing Company (BBC) and Samuel Adams beer, he was motivated by more than emulating his six generations of forbearers who were also brewmasters. Koch's goal was much bigger. He wanted to bring all of America a better brew, one that could compete on a world stage against the biggest names in beer: Anheuser-Busch, Miller, and Coors.

The effort required better ingredients—such as the expensive "noble hops" he imported from Europe at up to 20 times the cost of regular hops. It also necessitated the acquisition of recognized brewing talent—and Koch paid top dollar to hire the best brewmaster he could find. Then he started his business by filling a briefcase with bottled Sam Adams beer and walking it from bar to bar in Boston, seeking orders.

Koch was selling taste and quality. His product was not just beer but a beer-drinking experience. Even after the brand took off, there were no scantily clad babes in Sam Adams commercials, just a lot of guys drinking beer and having fun to a soundtrack of George Thorogood and the Destroyers playing "Who Do You Love?" Occasionally Koch would throw in a whimsical ad like the noble hops commercial, or an ad featuring a guy in patriot garb waiting by the side of the road to watch a Sam Adams beer truck pass. In that ad, the patriot delivers only one line to the unaware driver as the rig rolls by. In an emotion-filled voice he shouts: *"You* have the *best job* in the *world*!"

With the introduction of Sam Adams beer, Jim Koch established the first national craft brewing business in America. He was by no means the first craft brewer in the nation, but by creating a business that could hold its own against the majors on store shelves, he paved the way for many other craft brewers to follow him. Today, BBC is actually the largest brewer in America, mostly because of consolidations and the off-shoring of mainstream, noncraft brewers (including Anheuser Busch). Craft brewing is still a small business, relatively speaking. Koch's market share remains in the low double digits. But beer drinking has never been better, thanks mainly to Jim Koch.

Boston Brewing Company is worthy of transformative status because it didn't just succeed, it changed an entire marketplace. There were several things that played a role in the transformation, including Koch's direct marketing concept in the early days, and the product's colorful namesake (firebrand Samuel Adams was a brewer as well as a revolutionary patriot). Quality was undeniably important; the beer has won scores of national and international competitions over the years. But BBC would not have succeeded on such a grand scale had Koch not been thinking about greatness even when his business was smaller than small. Unlike many who came before him, including his own family, he refused to let the lack of known craft-brewing scaling methods stop him from going national. He was committed to transforming via a scalable process.

Companies that transform via process are farsighted, detail oriented, and structure conscious. They believe that how something is done is as, or even more, important than what is being done. They see the scaffolding of an emerging business and launch their companies with scaling in mind. While other fast-growth companies procrastinate on issues they view as secondary to simply pushing out the product and getting it sold, these companies expend time and resources to ensure that the essence of the company won't just survive expansion but will thrive on it. These founders and CEOs are planning from the beginning for a day long after they've moved into a different position, or even out of the company. They seek to put all the pieces in place at the very start so as to make the company run itself, no matter how big it gets.

In Jim Koch's case, there were several process-based decisions that were central to his success. First and foremost, he hired an indisputably top-notch brewmaster—the very one, in fact, who had invented light beer. This gave BBC credibility even before the first sip of Sam Adams was tasted by most would-be critics. Koch also eschewed traditional marketing and sales—Jim himself did most of that. Not afraid of vivid imagery, in one of our most colorful discussions he said: "The difference between sales and marketing is like the difference between sex and masturbation. One you do all by yourself alone in the dark and the other you do face-to-face with another person."

He did, however, invest in advertising. The purpose, or process, of his advertising was very specific. He believed that the best expenditure of his dollar was to educate the customer on what makes a great beer. The company's earliest ads were 60-second treatises on what goes into a great, super-premium beer, what a creamy head indicates about the quality of the beer, and various tasting tips not unlike what oenophiles share with one another in a winery's tasting room. It was all intended to teach a consumer how to recognize quality and demand it—if not from Jim Koch, then from another craft brewer. He was creating a category, not just a business.

Most importantly, Koch opted not to build a brewery, at least initially. This completely contradicted craft-brewing orthodoxy, which dictated that a manufacturing company must own its operations. However, Koch knew he could control quality by producing in underutilized breweries around the country. Recognizing the scarcity of his resources, this strategy gave Koch scale, flexibility, and, most importantly, control over the end product. If he were ever dissatisfied, he could simply threaten to pull a brewery's contract. Since quality was his sole differentiator in the market, this was an essential advantage.

Contracting out the production also had the immediate effect of extending the geographic reach of BBC. This was important, because Koch assumed he would have trouble cracking the existing beer distribution system, and he did. With distributed production, Koch could run his own trucks within various regions, and this proved to be another plus. Instead of shipping his beer to a distributor's warehouse, possibly to sit and become stale, Koch could have his brews available in any market in the country within 24 hours of leaving the assembly line.

With these distinct processes in place, Koch could now push his advantages, such as eliminating stale beer. Viewed by some as a gimmick when Koch announced it, establishing sell-by dates was actually a help to BBC's scaling goals. It publicly reinforced the notion that beer was a living substance whose quality degraded with time. It also removed some of the internal decision making (what to do with old beer and what constitutes old beer) that builds bureaucracies in emerging companies. Sell-by dates were another way for Koch to ensure a continuing and laserlike focus on the brewing and selling of quality beer.

Koch's passion for process came from an unusual place—his highly paid job as a Boston Consulting Group consultant. Notwithstanding a 140-year family history in the beer-making business, he began his career consulting for paper mills and chemical plants, all of it work that gave him a healthy appreciation for "the unromantic adherence to details, the nitty-gritty that leads to quality," he told *Inc.* magazine in 1995. In such environments, there are ways of measuring good work and quality output. He expounded further in that article: "For quality to have meaning, it has to have a definition. In manufacturing, quality means conformance to specifications. In that mundane sense, Samuel Adams is a beer that's consistently good, that therefore conforms to specifications, that thus has quality."

In this way, Koch was and is different from others in craft brewing. While others maintained their tiny and quaint breweries, or built carbon copies in key cities, limiting their production to ensure an experience—"because the experience is what the customers are buying," they reasoned—Koch made it all about the beer. The process he put into place ensured a beer-drinking experience that had nothing to do with atmospherics and everything to do with getting a fresh brew into every hand that wanted it, no matter where the drinker happened to live.

In this chapter we will consider other companies that, like BBC, have set a steady drumbeat of process for their people to step to. As you'll see, each company has taken a somewhat different approach to establishing its growth-enhancing processes. Some are quite rigid; others can be argued to be almost nonprocesses. Moreover, what some might call a process, others would refer to as a broad template of suggested ways of doing business, the following of which is dependent on culture, training, and group expectations.

Indeed, not all companies that transform via process achieve scale by building things, and some of the things that do get built are more virtual than tangible. So don't get sidetracked by the erroneous notion that transforming via process requires creating excess capacity to grow into. Koch scaled up by contracting with underutilized breweries, but he was never more than a one- or two-year contract away from being able to scale back. The companies that invest in bricks and mortar or highly built-out networks of various types take a bigger and far less flexible risk.

I think you'll see as you read the remainder of this chapter that the companies that transform via process have three things in common: a clear vision of a successful future, the recognition that growth can be as worrisome as it is welcome if not properly designed into the business model, and a sense that how a company does things ought to be an expression not just of who it is but who it intends to be.

SETTING LIMITS TO REACH HIGHER

Walk into any of Chipotle Grill's 900 locations in 33 states and you know what you're getting: really good fast food in an industrially clean but hip setting. You also know you're going to get exactly what you want, within limits. You can have a burrito or a bowl (a burrito with everything but the tortilla), a fajita burrito, tacos, or a salad. You choose your protein (pork, chicken, beef, or vegetarian), your beans, and your salsa. There are 65,535 different combinations possible—all stemming from just 17 ingredient options on the menu.

Just as it was all about the beer for Jim Koch, it's all about the food for Steve Ells.

Founder/CEO Ells has taken steps to ensure that Chipotle Grill avoids the temptation to try to be everything to everybody, as many fast-food chains do. What he has envisioned from the chain's Denver-area beginning is high-quality, restaurant-caliber cooking based on the best ingredients, spices, and cooking techniques. To him, focus is essential. Ells isn't going to stray into other cuisines or expand his south-of-the-border offerings. He has carved out a niche small enough to ensure excellence, and he's happy there—very happy, in fact. His restaurants are excitedly anticipated before they arrive and heavily patronized once they open. Many recent years have seen Chipotle's same-store sales grow at a rate of more than 10 percent per year, well outpacing competitors.

Chipotle Grill's limited menu, with its assembly-line production system, standardized cooking techniques and simple, replicable décor, have all enabled the chain's growth. Everything about the business is proudly formulaic. There's no internal debate about what to put on the menu, or whether to reflect local style in the design of the restaurant, or how to hire and train employees. It all comes down from corporate headquarters, and the result is a kind of uniformity of customer experience achieved previously only by the biggest fast-food chains—the McDonald's and the Burger Kings of the world.

Indeed, McDonald's perhaps thought it had found a kindred spirit in Chipotle Grill. The burger giant invested heavily in the upstart and, in fact, owned 90 percent of Chipotle Grill at the height of the relationship in 2001. It's no exaggeration to say that Chipotle Grill owes its deep market penetration to McDonald's end-of-the-century drive toward diversification—after all, McDonald's financial backing allowed Chipotle to expand from 16 restaurants in 1998 to over 500 in 2005. Nevertheless, McDonald's gradually found that Chipotle Grill was not a smaller version of itself. Chipotle Grill catered to young adults, not to families. It wasn't interested in establishing a low-priced value menu. And it wasn't receptive to McDonald's suggested expansions of the menu, including coffee drinks and desserts.

McDonald's and Chipotle Grill parted company in 2006, the same year that Chipotle went public. The burger giant's dissociation coincided with a back-to-basics move that saw several other acquisitions cut loose. But Ells has acknowledged a certain tension stemming from McDonald's oft-mentioned ways of expanding customer choices—all of which were nixed by Ells. For Denver's *Rocky Mountain News*, he explained: "We wouldn't do it better than anyone else and I don't want anything to be part of Chipotle that wouldn't be the very best."

What's notable, even surprising, about the Chipotle Grill story is the company's consistent ability to set boundaries. It sounds easy, but it's not, otherwise many more entrepreneurs and leaders of emerging companies would be succeeding at it. Experience has repeatedly shown that saying "yes" to every opportunity is extremely tempting for young companies, especially if the leadership hasn't already survived the school of hard knocks in a previous startup. Yet setting limits is crucial. And it is rare enough to warrant transformative status. Knowing what you do is one thing. Knowing what you *don't* do is rarer and much more important.

LETTING GO TO GAIN CONTROL

Can you imagine letting your suppliers call the shots on what you stock, how much of it you stock, and when to replenish supplies? E-commerce standout Zappos, which began as a shoe retailer and still does most of its business in that category, presents an interesting nugget to consider in any discussion revolving around process.

As you'll see in the upcoming chapter on irreverence, Zappos has a variety of reasons for being elevated to transformative status. It is certainly changing how shoes are sold, and it has established itself with a personality-forward sort of panache that few other companies have mustered. However, for the purposes of this discussion, I want to pause for just a moment to consider a heterodoxy: *You can transform via process without being a control freak.* In fact, you can often do a better job of establishing processes that enable growth and scale if you ease up on the reins—or even let go.

In the early days of the company, Zappos rapidly found that selection suffered and shipping delays resulted when the company tried to order its own merchandise from shoemakers. Now the company operates one of the most transparent supply chains in the e-commerce world. Via an extranet, major-brand shoe companies can see at a glance what's in stock at the Zappos warehouse, what's selling, and what needs replenishing. It is they who pull the trigger on the orders, suggesting to Zappos what to buy and how much of it. Furthermore, because Zappos represents more than one percent of all shoe sales industry-wide, the information that the e-retailer provides with the brands gives those brands a valuable planning tool for supplying other outlets.

To me, this is reminiscent of what Jim Koch did with Boston Brewing Company and Sam Adams beer. Just as Koch gave up the control of brewing to those who knew more about mass production of beer (the underutilized breweries around the country that Koch contracted with), the executive team at Zappos has given up control of shoe selecting, ordering, and inventorying to, well, folks who know more about it than Zappos ever will. Zappos has a process it can rely on. It doesn't have to maintain more than a skeleton staff to handle relationships with shoe manufacturers, allowing it to deploy its resources in ways more beneficial to customers. Shoe manufacturers receive an absolutely invaluable window into consumer demand that assists them in their own planning. In neither case did BBC or Zappos give up one ounce of close connection to the customer.

BRINGING THE DISTANT NEAR

When Cognizant Technology Solutions spun its outsourcing business out of Dun & Bradstreet, it was clear that perhaps the biggest challenge the young company faced was maintaining consistent service and clear communication between its American headquarters, the 75 percent of its workforce located in India, and the hundreds of corporations around the globe for which it provides IT solutions. It was a daunting task to try to create a closely inter-connected whole of what has grown to be 70,000 multicultural employees worldwide.

Cognizant has succeeded despite the odds. However, given how dispersed the organization is, the methods they use to stay coordinated may surprise you because they present less control rather than more. We'll focus on three of the major ones.

Cognizant University

Cognizant executives, led by CEO Francisco D'Souza, recognized from the outset that command and control would never work for such a far-flung and knowledge-centered operation. For this reason, they set about establishing what is now known as Cognizant University, a place tasked solely with "imparting the DNA of the company" to its new hires, as board chairman John Klein described it to me in a recent interview. As D'Souza put it in the same conversation: "Everybody who joins the company goes through about six months of training, give or take, depending on their position, yet in all circumstances they receive a very deep set of training on how we do things and how we expect things to be done. We also talk about the culture of the company and how we expect people to behave." Please note: The bulk of this training is about behavioral expectations rather than specific how-tos.

Certainly there are specifics about company policy and practice imparted in these sessions, but that's a relatively small slice of the training experience. Cognizant considers itself to be a values-based culture, so a significant amount of training effort goes into that "DNA" Klein speaks of—integrity, ethical standards, problem-solving methods, and assumptions regarding communications and transparency.

Therefore, even before the employees enter the field, they are grounded in the company's values, goals, and methods more than in the specific procedures for serving clients. This extensive and expensive commitment to training leads to Cognizant's trademarked method of working with corporate clients, known as "Two-in-a-Box."

The Two-in-a-Box Client Engagement Model

The "box" they speak of is the kind you'd find on an organizational chart. Cognizant client partners are embedded with the customer's own team, onsite, to ensure the best possible task alignment and interpersonal cohesion. The client partner shares his or her "box" with a senior Cognizant delivery manager located at any of Cognizant's global, nearshore, or local delivery centers. The two are empowered to operate on the customer's behalf almost as though they were running their own consulting company. Together, they are accountable for results.

What this means is that any given customer organization works with just one Cognizant team start to finish, with two key contacts interfacing with the customer as an extension of the customer's own staff. D'Souza considers Two-in-a-Box one of his most potent competitive weapons, and not just for its ability to center responsibility where it best belongs. "It also drives a great deal of collaboration across the enterprise," he told me. "It drives a unification of goals so [that] people have common, shared objectives. There isn't an 'us versus them' or a toss-it-over-the-wall kind of mentality. I think it's a tremendously valuable part of the organization."

In the conversation I had with D'Souza, he averred that if competitors were able to replicate Two-in-a-Box, they would have done so long ago. "In fact, a few competitors have tried to emulate it, but it's one of those things, that, unless you put it in early on, it's hard to retrofit an organization and an organizational culture to implement it—especially if another model has already taken hold."

D'Souza's offsite client managers regularly tell him that Two-in-a-Box helps them to deliver speedy solutions for their customers. "I was in a conversation recently with a team member who is managing our relationship with a large bank overseas," D'Souza said. "One of our competitors is also present, but we have the lion's share of the market there and he told me the simple reason is that he can make decisions much faster than our competition. 'Nobody is breathing over my shoulder when I make a decision,' he said. 'I have broad parameters. People tell me what I need to deliver and then I get to make decisions. My competitor, meanwhile, is always having to go back to his or her boss [to] figure out whether they can do something that is the right thing... for the client.'"

Of course, this autonomy is supported by modern collaboration tools. Using Web 2.0 technology, Cognizant client partners and delivery managers anywhere can be picking the brains of their coworkers, frequently in real time.

Cognizant 2.0, a Platform for Communication

Via Web 2.0 and social networking techniques that have become familiar and well-accepted with many of Cognizant's employees, the company has been able to establish an always-on system of worldwide communication known as Cognizant 2.0. The system allows employees *as well as clients* and business partners to share knowledge and assist one another with project-management issues. It's as simple as tossing out a question or a tip, and the aggregated brainpower thus made available is both a competitive advantage and a cost saver for customers.

Cognizant clients find that it's no longer necessary to expand a team to incorporate additional skills and problem-solving techniques. Finding solutions is no more difficult than updating one's status on Facebook. "We like to call it a virtual water cooler of 75,000 people who are all getting together on a minute-by-minute basis to talk about all sorts of topics related to work—and even some unrelated to work," Cognizant board chairman John Klein told me. "Having this many people around the virtual water cooler helps us build and reinforce [the] idea of a unified global corporation in a very strong and visceral way."

When I interviewed Klein and CEO D'Souza, I was struck by the motivator behind all the process and nonprocess Cognizant has instituted. "One of the things we measure or try to keep an eye on is talent density," D'Souza said. "What you find is that as the business becomes bigger and its complexity increases, the natural instinct to deal with that complexity is to introduce bureaucracy into the business to try to manage the complexity. [However], what happens when you introduce bureaucracy is that your talent density falls—because smart people don't want to work in such environments. We think a much smarter approach is, as long as you maintain your talent density at a high level, you don't necessarily need bureaucracy to manage complexity. You can do it with smart people who know what the right thing to do is."

Board chairman Klein agreed, but with one caveat: "You can do it only if you [have] not only...hired bright people but you have [also] spent the energy to really train them and impart the DNA to them as to how we make decisions, how we value customers, etc., so that by the time you delegate that responsibility and authority to them, they know exactly how the company wants them to handle things."

INCREASING TRUST WHILE INCREASING FREEDOM

Netflix is a company that, like Zappos, Amazon, Cognizant, and others, will make more than one appearance in this book. Founder Reed Hastings has created a company that displays its transformative nature in several different ways, including banishing small thinking, but it's worthy of mention here, especially in conjunction with Cognizant. Different as the two companies are, they have very similar motivations for the employee empowerment processes and nonprocesses they have put in place. Both seek to increase talent density in order to counter the increasing complexities of growth.

Early in 2009, an internal Netflix PowerPoint was leaked—or made to look like a leak—and it rippled across the Web. In it, Netflix laid out an employment manifesto of sorts, and it is notable for its thoughtful lack of detail.

In the slide set, Netflix describes a talent-centered business, one in which salaries are market aligned annually. There is no fixed budget for salaries and no annual raise pool to be divvied up. Netflix doesn't invest in career development, either, believing that surrounding each employee with "stunning colleagues" is sufficient.

Performance evaluation at Netflix consists entirely of "the keeper test": managers simply ask themselves how hard they'd work to keep any given employee, and if he or she isn't worth the equivalent of a cage fight, it's over.

As the company puts it, "Adequate performance gets a generous severance package." Yet talent alone isn't quite enough to ensure a long career with the company. "Brilliant jerks," are not welcomed, the company says, because "the cost to teamwork is too high."

But the freedom and responsibility section of the slide set is where Netflix and Cognizant converge. Netflix believes that "responsible people thrive on freedom and are worthy of freedom." Just as nobody is tracking working hours, nobody at Netflix is allotting or policing vacation time. The policy on vacation, then, is "There is no policy." It has been that way since 2004, with founder Hastings declaring that vacation tracking and face-time requirements on the job are "a relic of the industrial age." Neither is there a department policing travel or vetting expense reports or limiting business gifts given or received. The entire policy on such matters is, "Act in Netflix's best interests"—five words.

Netflix explains itself compellingly and in terms very similar to those that D'Souza uses when talking about Cognizant. *Netflix is seeking to be that rare organization that actually increases employee freedom as it grows.* Noting that most companies curtail freedom to avoid the errors that proliferate with growth, Netflix says it understands the motivation. But Netflix believes that rules and regulations drive talent out, taking innovation with it. Then, all it takes is a market shift of some kind to make the company irrelevant. Says the company: "Netflix prefers to grow not by proliferating rules but by proliferating talent." High-talent individuals can be managed more informally. Informality—or freedom—attracts more highly creative people. Therefore, Netflix sees the key to its success as nothing more than increasing the density of its talent faster than the complexity of the company can grow.

One of the ways Netflix pursues its goal is to eschew control for context. What that means is, instead of managers establishing rules and processes to ensure good performance, managers are responsible for creating the context in which quality work happens naturally. The only time to resort to command and control tactics, Netflix says, is when an employee is new and not yet up to speed enough to enjoy full freedom.

Like Cognizant, Netflix now finds itself a talent magnet. Recruiting has become almost effortless yet highly competitive, because Netflix's potential employees know that this is a place that provides maximal leeway to those who are guaranteed producers.

THE WISDOM OF NONPROCESS PROCESSES

The important thing to note about Cognizant and Netflix is that their employee empowerment strategies are as well thought out and relevant to their business models as are the internal production- or sales-oriented structures of Boston Brewing Company, Chipotle Grill, or Zappos. Each company has taken a look at what is required to scale the business, to guide it increasingly toward running itself, and to serve its clientele in the best way possible. With an intense focus on talent density, senior executives are free to focus more on long-term strategic planning, including the next-step function in their company's life. They know that the high-touch environment of a startup is short lived and not sustainable with growth. They build for an unknown, but hopefully prosperous, future. Most of all, they build for change.

Leadership books would have us believe that strong, involved leaders make for powerful companies, and it's often true. But it's only true when the leader has figured out how to guide without inhibiting and to inspire without goading. If we look at some of the huge and influential companies of past decades, we can see parables in some of them. Microsoft, led by the gatekeeping Bill Gates, soared until the chaos of the Internet required an equally helter-skelter approach to product development. As we'll see in a later chapter, Microsoft is attempting to reinvent itself into something more agile post-Gates.

When I think about entrepreneurs who have been able to grow their companies quickly and achieve enduring success, I find one thing in common: they all seem to recognize that what they are doing today isn't what they will be doing in six months, and it may bear no resemblance at all to what they'll be doing in six years' time. Nor can they be certain of a continuing role in all the change yet to come. This doesn't trouble them. They simply begin devoting time, energy, and resources to how they will make the necessary leaps from one stage in the company's growth to the next without needing to start over.

When you ask the CEOs of these transformative companies precisely how they do this, it's like so many of the aspects of transformation that we discuss in this book. They're at a loss to describe it. (In fact, D'Souza told me that he has quit trying to answer the question and instead asks his customers to characterize the difference for him.) From a leadership perspective, it's just the way they do things, and they say that they go about doing it without really thinking about what they're doing. I think they believe it, too. But I'm convinced there's more going on than meets the eye, and Cognizant's D'Souza metaphorically described it for me as that classic duck, all serene at the top, "but paddling furiously underneath."

Companies that are *built for change* in the category of process seek out the long view without ever forgetting what the company is today. They are very energetic and disciplined in how they analyze, plan, and structure things. Even if they expect to be with the company a long time, these CEOs proceed as though they won't. Instead of keeping everything in their heads, as most entrepreneurs tend to do, they know they must get their rationales and decision-making processes into other heads, if not onto pieces of paper. In short, they make it a key part of their mission to provide a template for the future based on the lessons learned from the present and the past.

If you've read the book *Made to Stick: Why Some Ideas Survive and Others Die*, by brothers Chip and Dan Heath, you may recall an experiment they cited. Students were given seven standard advertising templates within which to create ads for various products. The ads were then compared to a variety of different ads created by professionals, none of whom was given the templates. Surprisingly, the students created the better and more creative ads, and it was because the templates gave them a structure on which to build. The lesson, of course, is that whenever you impose some sort of structure or methodology or process, it actually frees people to be more successful—as long as the structure is more flexible than rigid, more talent enhancing than stifling.

Paying attention to process doesn't hamstring a fast-growth company; it actually frees it to do what it wants and needs to do. While a product-driven company experiences an identity crisis every time the market moves on, a process-driven company keeps doing what it has always done. It just does it with new results. Process-driven companies are truly *built for change*. It's not what they do that makes them who they are. It's how they do it.

Chapter 5

IRREVERENCE

For some, the Nataraja represents a dance of bliss, symbolized by an uplifted left foot. The dancing leg actually breaks the two-dimensional plane of the Shiva image; you can see that it's a little off-center. Transformative companies are often a little off-center, too. They dance as they work and laugh as they struggle, displaying an infectious irreverence—and a marked inability to take themselves too seriously. Like Shiva, they do a dance of bliss that spreads to all who approach, a dance that says "This is all a joke. We're in on it, and you can be too."

"Un-effing believable, they're now having toilet paper races on my flight!" a young woman says, speaking directly into her videocam.

She trains the lens on the front of the plane, where two stewards are explaining that the competition will pit one side of the aircraft against the other. "Right side is going to win!" our YouTube videographer shouts. Various right-siders make raise-the-roof or we're-number-one hand signals, while left-siders hiss.

At "Go!" each of the window-seaters in the front row takes hold of the loose end of a toilet paper roll and begins passing the roll backward. "Don't break the roll!" some chant, but these competitors, no fools, are leaving plenty of slack.

The right side wins and prize speculation ensues. "Uh, we don't need free drinks," our videographer deadpans into the camera. Free snacks are what these passengers will take away from the experience, but they'll also go home with a good story to tell—and proof once again that, at Southwest Airlines, it's not business as usual.

Southwest Airlines is a much-studied and indisputably transformative company. From its counterintuitive insight that low fares could lead to uncommonly high profits, it is that rara avis, the airline that does well year after year, even under the worst of circumstances. Southwest Airlines is valued at more than all other U.S. airlines combined. It also carries more passengers per year than any of its competitors.

There are many things that make Southwest Airlines *built for change*, but what has established and sustained its success is the company's irreverence. Only a highly irreverent company would create an environment where employees feel they can hold toilet paper races—or give their onboard safety briefing in rap, or sing "We Give You Peanuts," to the tune of the old torch song "(You Give Me) Fever." This is a company that understands the importance of fun.

However, more importantly, Southwest Airlines totally understands the value of not doing business as usual, which, to me, is the key point about transformation via irreverence. They don't pay obeisance to the existing norms of the way things are done. They make their own way. They do what's best suited to their goals in the marketplace. If that involves a little merriment and some nose-thumbing at convention, well then, so be it.

In this chapter we'll take a look at a few stellar examples of how companies transform via irreverence. We'll see that zany acts and weird traditions are only one way of expressing irreverence; there are others. We'll also see that however a transforming company opts to express its irreverence, there is always an underlying strategy that compels it. Invariably, the strategy requires being a different sort of company, one that thrives on employee individuality and creativity.

TAKING A GREAT IDEA AND MAKING IT FLY

The transformative idea behind Southwest Airlines was to bring fares down and get more Americans into the air. The carrier eschewed hub-and-spoke routes in favor of short hops and no stops, and, to reduce maintenance costs, it flew only 737s. In the 1970s, when Southwest began as a regional carrier in Texas, less than 20 percent of Americans had traveled by air. Nowadays, thanks to Southwest and the other discounters that followed suit, less than 20 percent *haven't* flown.

Nevertheless, the most irreverent action Southwest ever took was to eschew traditional tickets. To make its system of nonstop, point-to-point flights work, the airline needed to turn planes around on a dime. Tickets, they found, took too long to process at the gate. What's more, at $30 to produce and mail each one, they were expensive. Adding that fee to the fares would almost double the cost on some routes and risk Southwest's reputation as a low-cost carrier. Still, eliminating the multicopied affairs known as paper tickets would be a revolutionary move, because passengers were accustomed to them and would feel nervous going to the airport without one.

Then came the decisive moment. Responding to pressure from the major carriers that owned the leading reservations systems, travel agents began refusing to issue tickets for Southwest flights. The situation called into question the use of travel agents. What exactly did they do for Southwest, beyond generating and distributing tickets? Nothing, really, though without a travel agent, how would the passenger receive a ticket? The airline's options were either to develop its own front-end computer program and allow agents to print tickets for Southwest flights, or to eliminate tickets altogether.

Early in my career, Herb Kelleher once told a small group of us how Southwest stared down this challenge in one of the greatest moments of corporate simplification and irreverence I've ever heard.

Herb: "We were sitting in a management meeting trying to figure out what to do when somebody piped up and asked 'Do we really give a damn what United thinks a ticket is? Isn't it more important what *we* think it is?'"

"Reflexively," we all said 'No, we only care what we think a ticket is.'

"So then the manager says, 'Then why don't we just print out a single piece of paper that says "This is a Ticket?" Screw what United thinks!'"

And that's how those Southwest ticket kiosks came to be.

Subsequently, Southwest learned something important about not doing business as usual: Customers who have come to expect the unusual will adapt quite easily, even happily, to the next example of out-of-the-box thinking. Since passengers were already accustomed to no assigned seating and boarding passes that were only distributed at the airport—both things that Southwest had done to suit the idiosyncrasies of its business plan—ticketless travel seemed the next logical step. As we all know, the airline industry's current standard is e-ticketing, and it started with a willingness to disregard millions of dollars of imbedded infrastructure and time-honored ways of doing business.

Challenging the status quo, as Southwest has done repeatedly, requires a certain creative density in a company's employee ranks—especially as the company grows. But how do you screen for the ability to think outside the box? There are instruments that attempt to do it, but for an irreverent company such as Southwest Airlines, the answer has been: "Let them come to us." Because they do, in droves.

Aspiring employees come to the airline en masse because they know that at Southwest they can be extraordinary. They have seen that this company enjoys big, caring personalities with well-developed senses of humor—the toilet-paper races tell them so. Applicants vying for jobs know that if they get one, they will be able to express themselves in ways that few other jobs permit—and maybe end up on YouTube, too.

Singing and dancing employees don't necessarily draw raises, citations, or even kudos from their superiors at Southwest, but the appreciation is top-down, and more than implied. Consider what happens on Halloween: executives arrive at work in costume and employees present skits that are more lavishly produced each year. Does any work get done? "No. None at all," chief financial officer Laura Wright told the *New York Times* in February 2008. Adds CEO Gary C. Kelly, "I often get asked about a 'lost day' of work, but Halloween seems to re-energize our folks." So does the annual chili cook-off in April, another day during which the Southwest workforce plays.

Talk about finding joy in the dance of life—Southwest Airlines has institutionalized it. This is an airline that, from the beginning, portrayed itself as the fun way to fly, at first with stewardesses in hot pants and, later, with crew members in golf shirts and Bermuda shorts. But don't miss the hard-headed business sense that underlies the fun. The airline needs passenger volume, and it is brand loyalty that builds volume. The stakes in this effort are employee competence, but the crucial interface is at airside. Onboard employees need to be not only trustworthy in an emergency but also engaging with customers as well. That's not easy in a job that's numbingly repetitive. Being able to crack a joke, or sing or rap the announcement, well, that elevates the job to a performance. Southwest Airlines excels because management knows that to attract the most competent, but also the most joyful, people, they need to offer their hires freedom of expression. They must assure employees of the right to offer their competence in an individualized way. That's why most Southwest flight attendants love their jobs, and their passengers love to fly Southwest.

TURNING A CALL CENTER UPSIDE DOWN

Another company that enjoys fierce brand loyalty is the online shoe retailer Zappos. Like Southwest, Zappos has worked hard to build a relationship with its customers. In fact, the only thing it has worked harder at is building the corporate culture that makes relationship building possible.

A visit to Zappos' headquarters in Henderson, Nevada, is, by all accounts, an event. Portions of the office are employee decorated. In the section with a jungle theme, for example, software engineers identify themselves as bug killers, complete with mosquito netting, fly swatters, and aerosol bug bombs. Walking through the building you may be greeted by the din of squeaky toys, kazoos, karaoke-singing, or all of it at once. You might even catch one of the company's employee parades, which can occur almost daily for any reason someone can drum up.

Zappos celebrates the unconventional. It's the kind of place where groups of employees get together to write songs about the joys of online selling and then, after performing them for coworkers, upload them to the Web site for customers to see. It's also a place where tradition reigns, and the stranger the better. Each year as the Nevada summer begins to heat up, for example, the company conducts a gala head-shaving event.

Zappos has used irreverence, even zaniness, to transform a business that no one necessarily thought to transform: shoe retailing. It's irreverent in the spiked way that some associate with the word, but it's also irreverent according to the definition I prefer: it departs from the usual way of doing things, and it does so for the sake of something beyond nonconformity. Zappos might choose another word for it, but the company knows that irreverence is the key to the success it has achieved.

From a standing start in the late 1990s, founder Nick Swinmurn's idea and CEO Tony Hsieh's management strategy have combined to build a virtual shoe colossus. Nearly 8 million customers worldwide consider Zappos the best way to get a fix for a footwear addiction—and 40 percent of them are men. Zappos isn't a discounter; it's a full-price retailer that attempts to provide a shoe-store experience without the store. In actuality, Zappos is many stores combined. With 3 million pairs in the warehouse and almost 1,000 carried brands, it's the place to go if selection is your priority.

However, to think that Zappos is all about the shoes is to miss the point—and not just because Zappos has expanded into other product lines such as handbags, clothing, and cookware. The real product at Zappos is customer service. Zappos is well-known and loved for its 365-day return policy, its prepaid return shipping labels, and its habit of spontaneously upgrading orders to overnight shipping at no charge. The first of Zappos Ten Commandments is "Deliver WOW," and employees do just that. Some customers, in fact, have reported ordering shoes near midnight and having them show up on the doorstep mid-morning.

Here's a differentiator from other Web retailers: customers who prefer dealing with a real person aren't second-class citizens at Zappos. The site's phone number is prominently displayed, not buried, and those who call it find a rarity in online business transactions: actual assistance. The people at the other end of the phone line are not just order takers but folks who really want to help you figure out whether a "charcoal" shoe is more black than gray, or if this shoe has enough support for fallen arches. If Zappos doesn't carry the shoe you're looking for, the rep on the other end of the line will look for it elsewhere, because that's how Zappos defines customer service—helping customers find what they need as quickly as possible.

Still, these preorder conversations have been known to go on for an hour and stray far beyond mere shoe talk. That's fine with Zappos. Customer service representatives are instructed to be themselves, have fun, and, if possible, build a lasting relationship between the company and the customer. At least once, when the rep detected trouble in a customer's life, flowers turned up on her doorstep courtesy of Zappos. Now it's part of the lore of this company's anything-to-amaze philosophy. "What we care about," Hsieh told *Chain*

Store Age in 2007, "is that our associates go above and beyond the customer's expectations."

What happens when the inevitable mistake occurs? The relationship building carries Zappos through. The customer knows she isn't having a problem with a monolith; she is having a problem with a group of genuine people who collect bobble-head dolls and show off their tattoos on the company Web site. These aren't automatons in the customer's eyes. Customers know that if they bring a problem to a call center operator, that person won't hide behind nullifying corporate policy to avoid dealing with the issue. Instead, customers believe that they are more likely to encounter well-intentioned people who are determined to make things right. Even the company's "Sorry we can't fill your order" e-mails are written like personal letters of apology, signed by a real person, and sweetened with offers of $15 off the customer's next order.

Consider how counterintuitive that is. Zappos is, basically, a call center—phones and computers and people working them from cubicles. The mantra of any call center is speed, efficiency, and consistency. Typically, call center employees are evaluated by the number of calls they handle per hour or day, how well they stick to the script provided them, and whether they're able to sell up or sell more. There's nothing customized or individual about it.

What's irreverent about Zappos is that it throws away the dehumanizing script, the one that tells its people never to reveal themselves. While others with similar business models have come to believe the prevailing wisdom—namely, that customers want efficiency when ordering commodities like shoes—Zappos assumes that what their customers really want is a very human and connected interaction, a completely humane substitute for an in-store experience. This might not be true of all Internet shoppers, but—and this is key—it's true of the ones Zappos needs to make its business model work. Zappos's business is built on repeat customers. Hsieh learned the hard way that discount shoppers are not loyal. They are fickle, letting the siren call of reduced prices draw them hither and yon. Competing for these low-price shoppers requires a lot of drum-banging, and advertising to this group doesn't tend to be cost-effective. You're basically winning the same customers over and over again.

"You can get anyone to buy from you once," CEO Hsieh told *WWD* in November 2006. "The hard part is getting people to buy from you again and again and again."

That's why Zappos has adopted such customer-friendly shipping and return policies. Sure, these amenities cost money. Free shipping alone is estimated to cost $100 million a year. Indeed, "overly generous" is one of the kinder terms critics use to describe it. But Hsieh considers the dollars well spent. After all, Zappos has found that customers who return 25 percent to 50 percent of what they order actually spend more and splurge on pricier items when they don't have to worry about restrictive return policies. No doubt Zappos could get by with doing less for customers, but that wouldn't be wowing them. Doing more brings the wow and engenders loyalty. "Seventy-five percent of our sales are to repeat customers," Hsieh's longtime chairman and COO/CFO Alfred Lin boasted to *Fortune* in February 2009.

As we saw with Southwest Airlines, an operation such as Zappos rises or falls on the quality of its employees. Hsieh says he doesn't look for people who know shoes. He says he looks for people with passion, and that's a comment frequently heard from high-flying companies, especially ones I'd label as transformative. Google, for example, on its Web page titled "Life at Google," also touts its desire to find "people who are passionate about their lives." But I think these companies are actually looking for much more than passion. For many, passion is an impulse without action, an aimless desire. Irreverence at Zappos is the directed form of that passion—it's passion that is channeled into meeting customer needs and finding fun in doing so in ways that are anything but de rigueur.

For lack of a better term, Zappos hires "people-people," and this can be screened for. But interviewing and testing only goes so far. Typical hiring regimens won't tell you whether new hires can go more than skin-deep with their interactions, or whether they've got anything interesting to offer when they do. That's why Zappos takes it further. Job applications come with little cartoons and crossword puzzles and quips on them. Questions such as "What's your theme song?" and "What makes you weird?" are aimed at bringing into focus the applicant's personality. Nobody at Zappos cares whether the would-be employee knows anything about e-commerce in general or apparel sales in particular, but they do look for folks who play well with others. "We want people who are passionate about what Zappos is about—service," Hsieh told the *Washington Times* in 2008. "I don't care if they're passionate about shoes."

Getting hired is just the first big hurdle. New employees are then put through four months of training, and Zappos doesn't want to make that investment for nothing. The company wants to ensure that the fresh faces coming out of it really want to work for Zappos instead of merely collecting a paycheck. That's why the company takes the outrageously irreverent step of offering training graduates $2,000 to quit before they even start. There are very few takers. So few, in fact, that the quit payment has had to grow from the original $100 to today's $2,000 just to ensure that every now and then someone will take the bait. After all, this is a place where you can set your own hours, wear what you want, and enjoy some of the best perks around. Who wouldn't want a job with free lunch in the cafeteria each day, plus access to a nap room? Who wouldn't jump at the chance to participate in profit-sharing and enjoy fully funded health benefits with company-paid copays? There's even a life coach on staff to help employees sort through personal concerns that might be complicating their ability to be friendly on the phone. Hsieh says the guy easily pays for himself by reducing employee stress. But even that benefit is offered in a way that is more than a little tongue-in-cheek. Instead of lying on a couch to detail the woes of your life, as you would in a therapist's office, you are required—required!—to take a seat on a red velvet throne.

Despite the employee-centric culture, there are rules, including those Ten Commandments that must not be broken, and here are a few more of them:

> *Embrace and drive change.* Don't groan, "We've never done it this way!"
> *Create fun and a little weirdness.* Even firing offenses are explained through funny skits.
> *Be passionate and determined.* Share the things that you think make life worth living.
> *Be humble.* "Zapponians" can do worse than learn from CEO Hsieh, whose cool is the quiet kind.

Zappos strives to be a mutually supportive workplace where any employee can authorize a $50 bonus for a fellow worker who goes above and beyond the call of duty. Embedded in the protocol is an assumption that Zappos will become the center of an employee's existence—that, in some way, Zappos becomes family. Managers, for example, are strongly encouraged to spend 10 to 20 percent of their off-time with members of their team, doing fun things outside the office. Hsieh says he's convinced that the off-duty interactions improve efficiency when on-duty. By how much? The self-reported estimates from the teams themselves range from 20 percent to a credulity-stretching 100 percent.

The internal task for Hsieh as the company has grown is keeping Zappos weird. But there is also an external aspect to it, and that's bringing customers into the culture, making them feel part of the weirdness. It's something that Zappos does better than almost anyone else, online or off. It starts with the customer-service people on the telephone who are not only serving customers but also listening, laughing, and finding common interests. It continues online, where the Zappos Web site includes little homilies from the company life coach; employee-written ruminations on seasons, holidays, and favorite sports; photos from company events; a pet page; and the boss's own blog. Zappos sees itself reflected back in the form of exuberant, bubbly, self-revealing comments from its customers. They don't sound like reviews or thank-you notes. They sound like run-on letters from friends:

> I can't say enough about your team member. We chatted about Zappos and my order, and we chatted [about] the role Zappos played in a recent Celebrity Apprentice episode. She made me feel like we were old friends and what I appreciated a lot was the fact that I wasn't "bothering" her as so many employees these days make customers feel. We had many things in common, our family history with the automobile industry, the state of the economy, etc.... We both truly enjoyed our conversation.... The other day I received a post card from the same customer service rep with a personal note. She was hoping I was enjoying my new shoes and thanked me again for "allowing" her to assist me. The pleasure was all mine, my only regret is that I was too busy and hadn't had time to write this email regarding my experience. Sincerely, Janet E., May 2009.

Now, Amazon has entered the picture, with Jeff Bezos and company buying Zappos in the summer of 2009, investing $847 million and promising customers more of the same, only better. Time will tell if Zappos can maintain that irreverent customer connection.

MAKING BUSINESS A GAME

Despite many a puckish management consultant's best efforts, one of the enduring assumptions about business is that the numbers are the sole province of the C-Suite. A little data trickles down to middle management in the form of sales projections and goals, but the fine-grained stuff that really tells where corporate gains are made and lost might as well be a foreign language to those in the average workplace. But all this has begun to change over the last 25 years, thanks in no small measure to what happened at a little rebuilder of engines and engine components in Springfield, Missouri, known as Springfield Remanufacturing Corp. (SRC).

What CEO Jack Stack was able to create at SRC has become known as the Great Game of Business—it even became the title of a best-selling book. Stack is now a much sought-after speaker and ranks as something of a management guru in the world of emerging companies. He is known for popularizing open book management, wherein all employees, no matter how lowly, have both access to the key numbers that describe the condition of the company they work for and the power to affect them. Stack has shown many a corporate leader that while knowing your key numbers is important, empowering your employees to work with them and improve upon them is transformational.

The salient point isn't that Stack helped usher in a new era of quantitative management, though he certainly did that. The point is that Stack's story is quintessentially irreverent—and, in my opinion, is well worth revisiting from this slightly different angle. What he did at SRC shows us that irreverence truly is not a synonym for zaniness. Irreverence means throwing out the old playbook, not just for the fun of it—though fun is fine—but to meet the unique needs at hand.

SRC's needs were many and significant. It was a failing subsidiary of International Harvester (IH), losing $2 million a year on revenues of $26 million when Stack took over as CEO in 1979. Stack did what he could to improve matters while working within IH's system, but he didn't make much headway until he and a dozen employees banded together in 1983 to take over the company in a leveraged buyout. In so doing, they likely saved the company from eventual liquidation, because IH was among many heavy-equipment manufacturers hard hit by recession at that time.

Weighed down by SRC's debt, yet convinced of its power to recover, Stack did the only thing that made any sense to him—he began to track every dime and analyze every aspect of the company's performance. This didn't come easily for Stack; he was neither schooled nor trained in this sort of by-the-numbers management. Yet he and his team essentially produced an income statement every single day. Survival required it.

At the same time, Stack began to fashion a new kind of role for himself after the leveraged buyout. He understood that the traditional role of a manager was to tell his people what to do, when to do it, and perhaps even how to do it. But Stack wanted his employees to know why. And he didn't want to tell them why—he wanted the couple hundred of them to figure it out for themselves. As he told *Inc.* magazine in SRC's debut article back in 1986, "Why hire a guy and only use his brain to grind crankshafts?"

Stack also had another "why" question on his mind back in those early days: "I just felt that if you were going to spend [the] majority of your time doing a job, why couldn't you have fun at it?" Specifically, why couldn't the job be more like a game?

Soon the employee lunchroom had a flashing message board, and it said things like, "Fuel Injection Labor Utilization 98%." Maybe that meant nothing to employees at first, and maybe they didn't even care—until Stack coupled the information with reward. Soon they could tell anybody that the flashing message meant that SRC's laborers were almost entirely deployed on rebuilding fuel injectors. Almost nothing, just two percent of that labor, was going to overhead. Keeping their labor percentage high would make the workforce eligible for bonuses under a cumbersomely named campaign: STP-GUTR ("Stop the Praise, Give Us the Raise").

With money on the table, SRC became a transformed workplace. Soon employees were discussing numbers and asking for ever more sophisticated financial information. Stack ended up offering courses akin to those of a business school just to keep his employees interested in the game and, most importantly, able to win at it.

SRC won, too. In the years after the game began, sales grew at a rate of 40 percent per year. Net operating income rose to 11 percent. The debt-to-equity ratio plummeted from almost 90-to-1 to just over 5-to-1. The appraised value of a share in the company's employee stock ownership plan increased from 10 cents to $8.45, a stunning growth rate in a traditional industry. What's more, rates of turnover, absenteeism, and recordable plant accidents went from high to negligible.

The transformation was even greater than the numbers would suggest. Departments and divisions had learned to run themselves as small businesses, often setting their own budgets and strategizing their own goals. They made themselves accountable to each another as much as to their bosses. And they began to demand accountability from the top, too. Weekly progress company-wide was assessed at management meetings that became all-comers events, with attendees asking ever more incisive questions as their knowledge increased.

One company-wide event, described in that first *Inc.* story titled "The Turnaround," captures the spirit that Stack's Great Game engendered. After the assembled group watched a film clip depicting a Japanese challenge to competitiveness, Stack rose and said, "We have to do something about this, don't we?" The audience's cheers and shouts of "yeah!" just about knocked him over. Said one supervisor of that day, "I never knew working could be anything like this. It was great, simply great."

None of this sounds particularly amazing anymore, because there are many companies that have succeeded in marrying quantitative management with employee empowerment in SRC's wake. But Stack and company were the first to gain notice for abandoning business as usual to suit the particular needs of their workplace. Their irreverence didn't just save their company, it made SRC *built for change*. As SRC grew and learned, and related its experiences, it also transformed how many managers thought about driving profits and setting goals.

THE IRREVERENT PAYOFF:
COMMITTED EMPLOYEES

Southwest Airlines, Zappos, and SRC are just three well-known examples of transformation via irreverence. These companies represent various levels of customer contact and employee skill, and what they sell could not be more different. Yet one of the things they have in common—aside from their irreverent approach to business—is an uncommonly committed workforce. There's no chicken-or-egg question to be asked here. It's clear that these exceedingly loyal and energetic workforces were created by irreverent attitudes and practices. I think it's worth our time to think about the nature of this cause-and-effect relationship.

As we've seen, each of these companies depends upon a certain creative density to perpetuate its business model. Each needs employees who are willing and able to problem solve. Each has worked to establish an environment that empowers employees to seek information, to make judgments, and to become the best version of themselves on the job. Some of the talent was hired, no doubt, but most was developed onsite, through the unusual and status quo–challenging environment of these workplaces.

With their willingness to take an irreverent approach to fulfilling their business model, Southwest, Zappos, and SRC let the genie out of the bottle. They provided a taste of self-expression found at the heart of an entrepreneurial experience. Should any one of these companies grow tired of doing business irreverently, or be unable to maintain it across time and amid growth, the self-expression would wane and employees would move on to whatever more-irreverent environment they might find. They're not going to hang around if it means seeing that genie shoved back into the bottle.

Retention, then, is a big issue for the irreverent company. Doing what they're doing is almost enough, but not quite. To prevent Zapponians or Southwesters from finding the next cool workplace, or SRC folks from simply starting their own businesses, these irreverent companies must ensure that personal-growth needs continue to be met.

The ways of doing this are probably as numerous as the irreverent companies themselves, but I'll note some of the themes I've seen recur.

An All-Comers Approach to Internal Decision Making

We see this most readily at a place like Google, where brainstorming is the main method of advancing a new idea. As a result, a goodly number of Googlers are able to say they made an impact on operations within weeks of joining the company. It builds loyalty.

SRC, too, built its game on the input of the employees who know their own jobs best. The workers were the ones to identify process inefficiencies and waste. They were also the ones who decided which daily, monthly, and quarterly goals would best push profit to the bottom line. Furthermore, when corporate reports became available, employees were encouraged to make it their business to ask management tough questions about what the numbers meant.

Southwest and Zappos may not have the same kind of need for innovation or quantitative management as these other companies, but their openness to any and all input is obvious from what we see of the output.

An Abiding Respect for Individuality and Autonomy

Nobody is preapproving flight-attendant antics at Southwest Airlines. Nobody is telling Zappos employees that it would be a good idea to put out a call for customer-made videos of how they and their pets react to "box day," when the Zappos order arrives. Rules are few, and employees know that their creativity is not just tolerated but solicited. What's the limiter? Ultimately, there is only one, and I like how pharmaceutical company Astra Zeneca expresses it in the title of one of its e-learning modules. There, they call individuality and autonomy "Working for Your Inner Boss."

A Willingness to Make Mistakes

Irreverent companies roll with it, whatever comes. Both Zappos and SRC emphasize that there was no plan guiding their management choices. They say they didn't consciously set out to challenge the status quo. For them, there were only the realities of their respective markets and the trial-and-error learning that comes from looking for the approaches that work—be they managerial or strategic. That's all they could see: trials and errors, followed by more trials and errors.

Venture capitalist Vinod Khosla attributes this to company size, but it needn't be so. He asserts that the biggest advantage small companies have over large ones is that small companies are willing to tolerate mistakes. In other words, small companies are naturally more irreverent. They want and need to be scrappy, flexible, quick to initiate, and quicker to react when course correction is required.

A Well-Fertilized Field for Personal Growth and Creativity

Companies that know their irreverence depends on maintaining a certain creative density work hard to give it an opportunity to grow. Sometimes this can look like the company is just having fun or is trying to provide perks. However, bringing in lecturers or performers or encouraging cultural celebrations can play a contributory role in creativity, simply by adding diverse elements to corporate life. A creative mind does interesting things when confronted with a new idea, a challenging piece of art, or the quirky way that another creative person goes about his or her work. Exposure to new perspectives feeds the souls of employees and leads them to feel that their job is growing with them and vice versa—even if their title stays the same.

The ways of making fertile ground for creativity through diversity of perspective are limited only by the imaginations of top managers. For Southwest and Zappos, the sheer diversity of the workforce is enough to provide creative grist. For other companies, diverse perspectives are achieved by sending people to unusual conferences and seminars, just to see what's similar and different in that industry. Others might introduce their people to those who do the same job in a different context—just to let them talk and cross-pollinate.

Still others rely heavily on the arts for their mind-broadening attributes. One of the world's largest independently owned ad agencies, Wieden+ Kennedy, based in Portland, Oregon, stays fresh for top-shelf clients such as Nike by bringing in artists-in-residence who may introduce unexpected media, shapes, or color combinations to employees who may then use them to influence ad campaigns. Maybe that's not unusual for ad agencies; but, in reading about Wieden+Kennedy, I took special note of what this firm does to hang onto its most creative personnel. Founder Dan Wieden, for example, has been known to fund his staff's side ventures in film, books, and stage plays. He considers it an investment, though not precisely the kind you might think. "I want people outside to think, 'Geez, that would be a cool place to work,'" he told *Inc.* in 2004. "And I want the people already here to have a creative outlet—so they won't leave and go off to Hollywood."

PAY TO PLAY, PAY TO STAY

Irreverent companies recognize that the relationship they develop and maintain with their employees is—like everything they do—a challenge to the status quo. It's going to be a different kind of relationship because it *has* to be different.

Look once again at Zappos and its preemployment buyout offer, wherein new trainees are offered $2,000 not to start work. As I've said, it's completely irreverent. You don't pay people to leave before they start. But Zappos understands that there's a very interesting, implied handshake in every hire the company makes. Every now and then a would-be employee calls the bluff and it costs Zappos $2,000 to ensure that its entire workforce really and truly understands the company and welcomes being part of how it works. On the rare occasion when the company pays, it's noteworthy. But, looked at another way, it means that it's costing every employee—thousands of them—$2,000 to go to work for Zappos. They're turning down the cash. They're paying to stay. In essence, they're buying the culture. They're actively choosing irreverence.

Chapter 6

BANISHING SMALL THINKING

Shiva presses on the demon-dwarf Apasmara, declaring victory. With the force of one leg, Shiva has broken the back of a small but terrible adversary, thus allowing his dance to continue. From a business perspective, this dwarf signifies ignorance, indifference, and closed-mindedness. Transformative companies crush their dwarves by avoiding inertia and never becoming cowed by an unwillingness to take a fresh approach. They choose to reach high, see far, and *banish small thinking.*

It was in a decorous floating-boat restaurant in Amsterdam during the mid-1990s that David Huber found himself seated next to a senior Nortel marketing executive who, like Huber, was attending a European telecom conference. Despite their seating, they couldn't have been further apart.

All conference long, the buzz had been optical amplifiers—a technology that allowed telephone or cable companies to increase greatly the data-carrying capacity of their fiber-optic networks. Yet the Nortel executive at Huber's side displayed stereotypical big-company insouciance, and why shouldn't he? Nortel was the third largest communications equipment company in the world at the time and under no threat from any upstart technology or company.

"The Nortel guy told me he wasn't sure how big this was, or how important optical amplifiers were," Huber told me, recalling the evening in a recent conversation, "and I thought, 'This guy doesn't know what's going on.' He couldn't sort it out. He didn't have the insight to know what it meant, not even with all the tech people there at the conference trying to help him." Huber is a quiet man, but when we talked, he couldn't help but chuckle at the irony of it. This technology was one of the few major breakthroughs that led to the logarithmic growth of the Internet, but "The guy couldn't see the economic ramifications."

In 1997 optical amplifiers became the technology behind what was then the hottest initial public offering to date. Ciena Corp., Huber's company, raised $3.4 billion that year. I was among a group of early investors in Huber's company, and we made 100 times our money in just three years. It certainly changed my life, but it was nothing compared to what Ciena did for the technology of the Internet. Without Ciena, transporting terabytes of data simply wouldn't have been achieved with the same alacrity or in as short a period of time. Eventually, bigger companies caught up, but Ciena was the undisputed breakout.

The Nortel representative in Amsterdam wasn't the only one who had failed to see the opportunity, as Huber recalls. As a physicist at General Instruments (GI), Huber had gone to his bosses in the 1980s with excitement, urging them to invest heavily in this new technology. But GI had other things on its plate—an expensive leveraged buyout, for one thing, and a huge investment in copper-based transmission that was hard to turn away from. Most importantly, they thought of themselves strictly as a cable company, not a communications company, forgetting that at the technological center there was no real difference. Assuming that the technology would make too small a contribution to warrant the distraction, GI executives gave Huber the patents and wished him luck.

Huber thinks most of the major companies in telecommunications at the time would have done the same. "Industry-wide, people on the business side didn't fully appreciate the transformation." That's an understatement. Many companies would spend the next decade trying to reclaim a relevant role in the growth of the Internet through optical amplifiers and related technologies. Some caught the wave, but most didn't.

There are consequences to thinking small, as the Ciena story shows. You miss opportunities—in this case, a lock on the building blocks of the Internet in its inchoate phase. You stand to lose valuable people. You fall short of greatness, due only to comfort with the old and fear of the new. These attitudes keep near-term profits marching steadily and predictably upward. The cow keeps producing the cash. But inevitably the company ends up missing its future.

In this chapter we will take a look at companies that habitually banish small thinking. As you'll see, it's a difficult task that transformative companies manage to make look easy—with results that appear serendipitous.

THE RIVER AT THE CENTER
OF THE WORLD

"Amazon" seems a strange name for a company built on selling books—until you consider the meaning. The Amazon River of South America is the largest river in the world, carrying more volume than the next eight largest rivers combined. It also drains that water volume from the largest river basin on the planet.

Choosing such a name tells you quite a bit about Jeff Bezos, the perfervid founder and CEO of Amazon.com. It suggests he knew from the start that eventually he would be selling just about everything that can be sold and dominating e-commerce with a surging river of goods and services. From the beginning, he was thinking big.

Banishing small thinking seems to come naturally to Bezos, and, as a result, Amazon continually surprises and often confounds its most ardent supporters. Scarcely a month goes by without a business journalist wondering what Amazon is up to. It's nothing new; the collective head scratching has been going on since the company's founding in 1995.

First it was, "Does Amazon really think it can replace bookstores?" Then it was, "Why is Amazon letting used-book sellers compete on Amazon's own site?" And that's how it's been, month after month, year after year—from Amazon's decision to add nonbook consumer products, to its introduction of the Kindle reader, to its unexpected decision to market some of its surplus computing power and distribution apparatus to unaligned businesses. The critics always seem to be asking, "What is he thinking?"

In its early years, Amazon was a tragicomedy: how could a company that had yet to post a profit be regarded as a winner? As each quarter failed to drop so much as a penny to the bottom line, investors were forced to suspend their disbelief over and over again. But, amid the frenzied dot-com boom, Amazon's stock defied the naysayers. It hit a stratospheric $361 per share just before its three-for-one split in 1998. In a high-flying era, no dot-com company flew higher.

Then the dot-com crash hit hard, putting Bezos' face on a target again. Wall Street criticized him for bad timing and poor judgment. With 20/20 hindsight, they chastised him for the dot-com investments he'd made in failures such as pets.com, and especially for having built five separate $60 million distribution and shipping facilities—all for a company then doing just $1 billion in business. People started calling it Amazon.bomb.

Bezos acknowledges that many of his turn-of-the-century investments in dot-com companies were a colossal waste of capital, but, he notes, "the fundamentals of our business continuously improved" during that period. He further told interviewer Peter Burrows of *Business Week* in 2008 that his dot-com dalliances "didn't take us off our mission."

And take a second look at those expensive and superfluous warehouses Bezos built in the dot-com era. Not even his own management team wanted him to build the last of the five facilities. But these high-tech warehouses have given Amazon excess capacity during many holiday seasons, and they've allowed Bezos to create Fulfillment by Amazon, the newest effort to create a multiseller marketplace on its Web site. Smaller enterprises can store their inventories with Amazon and let Amazon handle shipping for them. In exchange for the business, Amazon lets the sales qualify for free shipping, which tends to increase the little guy's sales. What's in it for Amazon? It's another way to prevent stocking- and shipping-related glitches in the customer experience. Now even big, brick-and-mortar retailers like Target are signing on.

Bezos banishes small thinking by dutifully serving two longstanding masters: his obsession with customers and his focus on a long-term view of the future. He devotes relatively little energy to the near term and almost none to watching the competition. He recognizes benchmarking against competitors for what it is: a habitual tic that keeps a company doing what it knows is safe.

To fix his gaze on a more exciting future, Bezos purposefully looks backward. Each year he sends out his 1997 letter to shareholders, just to remind himself and everyone else of Amazon's founding propositions. The message in that gesture is: everything has changed, but really, nothing has changed.

The letter is an interesting read. In a section titled, "Obsess over Customers," we see what has grown only more true with time: that book selling was merely the vehicle that Amazon rode into the market. Bezos writes, "From the beginning, our focus has been on offering our customers compelling value."

"We realized that the Web was, and still is, the World Wide Wait. Therefore, we set out to offer customers something they simply could not get any other way, and *began serving them with books.*" Under "It's All about the Long Term," Bezos issues a promise to "invest aggressively to expand and leverage our customer base, brand, and infrastructure as we move to *establish an enduring franchise*" (all italics are mine).

As the preceding makes clear, Bezos is playing a very long game. He's the kind of guy who put his chips on China in spite of its poorly developed transportation and financial structures, cobbling together a network of bike delivery people who handle cash transactions at the doorstep. He's the kind of guy who tells customers they can have all the free, two-day shipping they want if they pony up $79 per year for what he calls Amazon Prime—and prepares to wait for their additional purchases to pay him back. Moreover, he's the kind of guy who spends three years and untold millions developing his entry to a market that most people had begun to write off: digital reading devices.

Bezos doesn't expect his ideas to make immediate sense to people, much less make money in the short term. He is content to bide his time and tune out the critics, often for five to seven years. Here's Bezos' simple disclaimer, as delivered to interviewer Burrows in the 2008 *Business Week* article: "We don't claim that our long-term approach is the right approach. We just claim it's ours."

A lot of the pushback Bezos felt from the investment community, especially in the early years, related to his continual habit of ignoring one of the cardinal rules, which goes something like: if you're not making any money, don't take any risks. Bezos banishes this idea as the small thinking that it is. "One of the only ways to get out of a tight box is to invent your way out," he maintains. Lacking advertising dollars early in Amazon's history, Bezos opted to create the Associates program, which allowed any Web site that linked to Amazon to receive a share of the revenue driven to the site. The move seemed bold at the time, and it was. But, more than that, it was seminal in building the site and driving it toward profitability.

THEY DIDN'T NAME IT "DVDs BY MAIL"

Just as Amazon's name tells us something important about the online retailer's aims, so should Netflix's moniker. As founder Reed Hastings has pointed out to *Money* and other media outlets over the years, "We didn't name it DVDs by Mail." From the beginning, Hastings was looking to have a wholly Internet-based future—one in which people could go online and select from far more movies than they could ever find in a store, and get them faster than snail mail could deliver.

Like Amazon, with its "Customers Who Bought This Item Also Bought" recommendations, Netflix endeavors to improve its customer retention and solidify its market position by predicting what its customers will enjoy. The recommendations are based on the customer's previous movie selections and ratings. However, for quite a while, the company hasn't been convinced it had the right predictive algorithm. Its engineers and software developers spent years trying to develop a new and improved system of recommending movies to customers, but to little avail.

What happened next is a great example of banishing small thinking.

Instead of considering its unsolved problem a proprietary issue that required the allocation of more internal resources, Netflix decided to do its business in the street. It didn't opt to hire more engineers and devote more costly time to the project; it decided to ask for outside help and wait to see what might materialize. The movie-rental company established the Netflix Prize—a contest to see who could solve the problem for the company.

Over three years and several prize-driven phases, the project moved toward completion, involving hundreds of developers worldwide. In September of 2009 the company announced it had a winner, a combination of two teams calling themselves BellKor's Pragmatic Chaos. The entry came in during the last half-hour of the contest, beating a second team's submission by 24 minutes. When the victors gathered to accept their award, it was the first time any of them had met in person. Their brains were simply the parts that came together to produce Netflix's crowd-sourced solution.

After the check was presented, Netflix founder Reed Hastings explained the business value of the winning submission in a video embedded on the Netflix Prize's Web site. "For most people, it's about one out of three movies they watch that they really love. We're trying to change that so it's two out of three movies they just rave about." With the prize, which set out a goal of improving the predictive algorithm by ten percent, "we engaged the research community to help us make that dream more and more a reality—because we know that the more people love movies, the more they watch. And the more they watch, the more they love Netflix and stay with Netflix."

IT and business bloggers alike have hailed the Netflix competition as the wave of the future, a stellar example of collaboratively combining diverse skills and ideas. The best summation of that collaboration came from the administrators of a Web site for the Midwest entrepreneurship conference Think Big Kansas City: "The [top two] teams beat the challenge by combining teams and their algorithms into more complex algorithms incorporating everybody's work. The more people joined, the more the resulting team's score would increase. In fact, teams that had it basically wrong—but for a few good ideas—made the difference when combined with teams which basically had it right, but couldn't close the deal on their own. Ironically, the most outlying approaches—the ones furthest away from the mainstream way to solve the given problem—proved most helpful toward the end of the contest." This blog's conclusion? "Next time someone says 'don't talk to a stranger'—tell them you can think of a million reasons to ignore them!"

Netflix has let it be known that the contest not only met their expectations and came in cheaper than if they had done the job in-house, but it also uncovered some new ideas that could improve their business model.

INTUIT BETS THE FARM

As we've seen, caution and mistaking what one believes to be one's own interest are the time-honored reasons for thinking small, and small thinking is the foundation of dilatory action. Companies worry that investors and shareholders will punish them for risks that don't pay off, and this fear is especially prevalent when the company isn't faring well. We've already seen that GI fell prey to this kind of hesitation and that Amazon proudly doubles down in the face of trouble. Intuit, the financial software giant, offers another great example of using hard times to bet big.

In 1986, when Intuit sought to achieve mass-market acceptance for its groundbreaking financial management software, Quicken, the company was three-and-a-half years old and had just survived a very lean period. "When I came to the company, they had [just] downsized from seven employees to four. The rental furniture went away and the dorm stuff came back," former Intuit CFO Eric Dunn told me. "The company was living hand-to-mouth."

Intuit had made its first splash in the market by doing something that originated with Intuit and has become commonplace today—designing software with customer needs in mind. Programmers actually interviewed customers in software stores. Sometimes they even followed select customers home to see exactly what sort of data-management needs they had and where the then-current products were failing them. But Intuit's original marketing and distribution model, selling through banks, had never really caught on. Just as management was seeing the need for change, Intuit was getting ready to launch a new version of Quicken for the Apple II. If ever there were a time to go for mass-market acceptance, this would be it—but how?

The then-traditional method of getting your software product into the hands of consumers was to sell to wholesalers, who, in turn, got the software into stores. There, knowledgeable employees would recommend the product to customers seeking a particular kind of solution. Intentionally or not, it kept software developers and their customers at a remove. But Intuit had watched Borland launch Turbo Pascal and Sidekick by advertising directly to consumers with wordy, features-oriented ads. The consumers then went to the stores and asked for Borland's product, bypassing the gatekeepers at the wholesale level and forcing stores to stock the software. Could this work for Quicken? There was at least one faction at Intuit that thought it could.

Unfortunately, money was an issue. Intuit had managed to scrape together a nest egg of about $100,000. It could be spent on the launch, but once it was gone, it was gone. If the expenditure wasn't sufficient to win Quicken the breakthrough it needed, it would likely be the end. Cooler heads argued that the smart bet, the familiar bet, was to play it safe and run a small-scale test of the direct-marketing concept first, but fortunately they were unpersuasive.

Bigger thinking prevailed, and, according to the authors of *Inside Intuit*, the definitive company history, Intuit went for it, risking the whole game on a single roll of the dice. "Let's either go out in a blaze of glory and get on with our lives after three-and-a-half years of struggle, or grow big," cofounding engineer and programmer Tom Proulx said. "We don't want to continue existing as the living dead." The company bet its entire net worth, plus every cent it was projected to earn that quarter, all on a $125,000 direct advertising campaign that would run only in the three leading computer magazines of the day. "End Financial Hassles," the ad was titled.

Fearing that ads alone might not be enough to capture the PC market for its financial software, Intuit made two more choices that only hindsight would prove either brilliant or entirely improvident. They cut Quicken's price from $99.95 to $49.95, hoping to attract impulse buyers, and, in an even bolder stroke, they removed the copy protection—allowing buyers to make copies for friends. The hopeful hunch was that customers who tried Quicken would like it and pass it on to others who would also like it and get hooked on it. Intuit wouldn't make any money from them at first. But the payday would come in the future, when these nonpaying customers would buy future upgrades and new releases—at least that was the risky bet Intuit was making.

It worked. Dunn remembers the excitement as the phones rang off the hook, each call bringing in at least one $50 sale. The big gamble had paved the final few miles of Intuit's rocky road to prosperity. After that, "there was a three- or four-year period there where the company roughly tripled in revenue every quarter," Dunn told me, clearly savoring the memory. He laughs. "When it began to slow, at like $33 million, we thought maybe we'd done something awful."

Intuit had one more memorable opportunity to test its mettle with big thinking. It was in the early 1990s, when Microsoft came sniffing around its financial-software niche. While speculation raged as to whether Gates and Company would launch a personal finance package of its own for Windows or partner with Intuit, Intuit received a visit from a Microsoft product manager. He didn't waste time getting to his proposal. Microsoft wasn't interested in any partnering arrangement, but the company was prepared to license Intuit's Quicken at a royalty of seven dollars per unit. "We were making $30 a unit, so we were aghast, insulted, livid—polite but *livid*," Dunn recalls. "We were a 200-person company and, with that deal, we'd be a holding company with twenty employees inside a year."

The fear was well-founded. Intuit had watched WordPerfect lose the word-processing market to Microsoft, and also saw the same fate meet Lotus when Microsoft cast its eyes upon the spreadsheet business. Once again, the very survival of Intuit was in question. DOS was going away, taking Quicken for DOS with it and leaving Intuit with only Quicken for Mac—a tiny 10 percent of Intuit's revenue. Microsoft seemed determined to create its own financial software for Windows if it couldn't scoop up Intuit's. And now, Microsoft, with its overtures to Intuit, had both a head start on Intuit and perhaps even some inside information on Intuit's approach to the software.

Small thinking would have indicated that Intuit should just cut a deal, but cofounder Proulx quite famously ground his heel into the carpet and said, "We will crush them!" when asked by board members how Intuit intended to respond to Microsoft's challenge. Dunn declaims the bravado. "We had a hard period and it was a strengthening period," he reflected during one of our conversations. Intuit elected to turn down the licensing deal and move forward with development of Quicken for Windows. Dunn shuttered himself into a Monterey condo with a development team and went to work.

We know the rest. Quicken for Windows became a best-seller. Microsoft Money, the intended usurper, quietly left the product shelves by the turn of the century, never having really dented Quicken's dominance.

Dunn attributes Intuit's apparent willingness to banish small thinking to a mixture of pride and determination. "We felt we deserved to be ranked with the big players in the financial-software industry." (Forty players had preceded Quicken to market.) "But we felt like outsiders, like the poor kid looking in the store window." Intuit did what it did, Dunn says, to escape its underdog position. "The underdog exploits niches and is creative and outmaneuvers the big guy," he told me.

True, and we both know that, in so doing, the transformative underdog clears away ossified thinking and gets the best ideas up and implemented quickly.

FOR GOOGLE IT'S MY WAY
OR THE HIGHWAY

Whether motivated by arrogance or brilliance or just plain audacity, the founders of Google have built their empire and changed our world by banishing small thinking at every major decision point.

The original math project that birthed the search engine started with studying Web links backward to see who was linking to what. It wouldn't have been necessary to look at the entire Web; it would have sufficed to cordon off a part of the Web to study how owners of Web pages could know who was linking to them and for what purpose. With the project he named BackRub, this is in fact what Google's eventual cofounder, Larry Page, took on—cataloging the entire Web. That, certainly, is where Google's big thinking started, but there was much more to come.

Consider a list of the search giant's more audacious moves:

- Said no to branding expenditures in favor of building buzz through public relations—at a time when other Internet startups were spending up to $120 million a year on marketing.
- Eschewed pay-to-play searches that mixed ads with actual results, even turning down a lucrative merger with GoTo.com at a time when Google desperately needed revenue—all because GoTo sold keywords to the highest bidder.
- Raised its first $25 million in 1999 from two of the biggest venture capital firms around—Sequoia Capital and Kleiner Perkins. Page and

cofounder Sergey Brin talked the financiers into taking the deal together and putting one man from each firm on Google's board of directors. The financial world gasped at the unprecedented arrangement.

- Launched AdWords, a means of selling keywords but keeping the ads separate from search results. AdRank employs a highly democratic means of deciding who gets top billing: whoever gets the most clicks gets the top spot, no matter how little the client may have paid for its keyword. These innovations put Google in the black and kept it there, creating the long-sought revenue source that search engines desperately needed.

- Created AdSense, in which Web sites agree to feature Google advertisers—and then pocket a few cents each time someone clicks on an ad.

- Syndicated AdWords to AOL, guaranteeing substantial revenue to AOL. Had the gamble failed, Google could have owed AOL enough money to run Google out of business. But the risk paid off, and the gutsy move made Google a major Internet player and, not incidentally, made it some money. In 2002, while most of the dot-com world was still on its knees, Google was the only one still hiring people and holding corporate parties.

- Hired its first CEO after 18 months of exhaustively interviewing some 75 candidates, and then assigned the winner, Eric Schmidt, to work as part of a triumvirate with Page and Brin. This meant, of course, that the founders would hold veto power over their CEO.

- Went public via Dutch auction, selling $2,718,281,828 worth of shares—a mathematically significant number that seemed intended only to declare nerd victory over the world. The unusual initial public offering document filed with the SECset out "An Owner's Manual for Google Shareholders" in which Page outlined how he, Brin, and Schmidt would run the company. "Google is not a conventional company. We do not intend to become one," the S-1 declared. The founders and Schmidt went on to establish a dual-class shareholder structure in which founders and senior executives would own shares 10 times more powerful than those sold to common shareholders. Like a family-owned media company that wants to protect its news-reporting from outside influence, Brin, Page, and Schmidt felt the structure was necessary because others would, as they put it in the Owner's Manual, "jeopardize the independence and focused objectivity" that marked Google's past and would be considered "most fundamental for its future." Oh, and Google wouldn't be predicting earnings for Wall Street. Neither would it engage in revenue-smoothing to suggest a less-than-realistic pattern of growth. Investors may have fumed, but they didn't balk. After all, Google's operating margins were running at more than 60 percent.

Google is still banishing small thinking. One of the company's current goals is to scan every book ever written to advance its corporate mission of "organizing the world's information."

As mentioned in Chapter 1, Google is a book unto itself. Fortunately, the definitive work has already been written in blogger-author Jeff Jarvis's *What Would Google Do?* In it, Jarvis pushes Google past being merely a verb and turns it into a full-fledged metaphor for how a company should think, invest, interact with customers, and engage the world at large.

FREEZING THE GATEKEEPERS

As we have seen, there are various reasons why transformative companies banish small thinking, and many versions as to how. When I consider some of the reasons *why* these companies are successful in thinking big, I consistently return to one thing: they find ways of holding internal naysayers at bay. If it's gatekeepers who slow down the traffic of bold ideas, these companies apparently find ways of fencing them in. If it's devil's advocates shooting ideas down "just for the sake of argument," something cultural seems to happen to keep such people from doing damage.

Even the biggest businesses recognize these challenges. David Hsieh, vice president of marketing at Cisco Systems, is quoted as follows on the online business resource BNet: "Big companies have a tendency to eat their own children. They [become] afraid of disrupting their own revenue stream with a new unit, or someone has a great idea and an executive sponsors it, but the moment the sponsor comes under pressure, they ditch all the little initiatives [and] focus on their core business." Cisco established an Emerging Technologies Group to give new ideas the protected environment they need to grow. Continues Hsieh on BNet, "The advantage of a new unit is to insulate it from people who say, 'We can't do it that way because we've done it a different way for years.' You want to enable a group of people to think more broadly and creatively without outside pressures."

The biggest proponent of cutting devil's advocates off at the knees—basically outlawing their existence—is IDEO, the noted innovation and creativity consulting firm based in San Francisco. In their book *Ten Faces of Innovation: IDEO's Strategies for Defeating the Devil's Advocate and Driving Creativity throughout Your Organization*, authors Tom Kelley and Jonathan Littman allege that "the devil's advocate may be the biggest innovation killer in America today." They say that when someone nonchalantly says, "Let me play the devil's advocate here," they're holding themselves harmless for the idea-wrecking negativity they are about to unleash. With this innocuous phrase as a shield, they take no ownership of the suppositions they raise. What's more, the tacit assumption is that the person whose idea is being criticized should take no umbrage. "I was just playing the devil's advocate," the critic will protest, as if suggesting that the naysayer had done the idea-generator a favor.

BUBBLING UP FROM THE BOTTOM

One additional trait that all of these companies, indeed all the companies in our study group who banish small thinking, possess is a policy that requires long-term (i.e., greater than one year) planning at very low levels in their organization. Consistently, three-year plans or longer, rather than quarterly or annual goals, were required of employees two and three levels below their less transformative peers. In contrast to more short-term-oriented businesses that only engage in long-term planning at the senior executive level, if at all, these companies expect that all thinking, planning, and executing—even at the lowest levels—will be for the long term. If GI had taken steps to fence in its gatekeepers, silence its devil's advocates, and listen to the organic long-term planning being done by David Huber and others, perhaps it would have had a multi-billion-dollar new business instead of divesting it for a pittance to Huber.

Transformative companies prevent these kinds of mistakes. They move aggressively to capture opportunity and give their ideas and enterprises time to develop, as does Amazon. They boldly expose their problems as a means of finding solutions, as does Netflix. They think well outside the box when trying to gain market attention and competitive advantage, as has Intuit. And, like Google, they do not hesitate to write their own rules, because after all, they know it's their game to win or lose. So, they think big.

Chapter 7

APPETITE FOR DESTRUCTION

The flame or *agni* in Shiva's upper left hand symbolizes destruction, the key function of this god, who is often called the Destroyer. Transformative companies have an *appetite for destruction*. They recognize that all business models are subject to being cast aside, if not completely blown up. But this is not destruction for destruction's sake. The consuming flame is balanced by the drumbeat of the creative process, as represented in Shiva's right hand. The old ways of doing business must die to allow the birth of what is new.

Craigslist versus newspapers, *American Idol* and Apple versus the music industry, and Amazon versus not just the book industry but the very idea of the book itself. Epic match-ups, all of them. In each case, it's a single entity taking down not just a competitor or two, but an entire category of adversaries. In this chapter we'll look at what drives companies to this sort of wholesale remaking of markets and industries. We'll examine how companies with an appetite for destruction are changing the culture around them. Perhaps most surprisingly, we'll find that in many cases this sort of depredatory behavior isn't motivated simply by the need to conquer, or to make more money than other enterprises, or even just for the bragging rights of having changed the world a bit. No, the urge to go forward with something revolutionary derives from the same origin that any great quest comes from: a burning desire in the heart. It's the love of a great idea, an intense passion for the customer, a seething frustration with the status quo or the undeserving louts who control it, and a belief that the company is uniquely suited to creating a better reality.

For a company to transform an industry in the true sense—sated only by completely substituting its product or service for that of the incumbent—an established business model must fail. Often, ensuring that a sitting technology or strategy fails is the force that drives the emergence of a transformative company; it is its raison d'être.

The eradication of a business model can be jarring—and we should be glad of it, says blogger-author Jeff Jarvis, author of *What Would Google Do?* In a recent seminar, Jarvis boiled down the merit of having an appetite for destruction to just three words. "Innovation yields efficiency," he maintained, noting that Google has upended search and revamped e-mail, to name just two of its many and continuing conquests.

There are also transformative companies that arise with little or no conscious thought of destroying anything. Many, in fact, at least want to appear blissfully unaware of the havoc their entry has caused. In this chapter we'll look at a variety of motivations, all leading to the same result. We will start with those that seem most benign.

THE ACCIDENTAL SUCKER PUNCH

It's unlikely that Craig Newmark woke up one morning and thought "I think I'll destroy the print newspaper business model today." Still, that's exactly what Craigslist has done.

By cleaving off one of the three main components of newspaper economics—classified ads—Craigslist has forced newspapers to survive with what they can earn from display advertising and subscriptions. As you may imagine, there's a limit to what newspapers can charge for subscriptions, especially if they want to maintain the broad and loyal readership that attracts commercial display advertising. Some estimates state that, based on its current cost structure, the *Washington Post* would need to charge subscribers $75 per issue if they based their model exclusively on display ads and subscriptions.

However, like subscriptions, display advertising is another wobbly leg. Newspaper advertising revenues have been dwindling for a generation, the decline sharpening with each bump in the business cycle. The result? Print newspapers have lost billions of dollars in profits over the past decade alone. Some publications in two-newspaper towns have idled their presses; others—even those that are pillars of American journalism—seem to be headed in the same direction. In fact, the outlook has become so grim that many journalistic insiders are suggesting that perhaps the only way print newspapers can survive is by going nonprofit.

Given all that destruction, it's hard to argue that Craigslist hasn't been transformative—though the site surely doesn't make it look like anything special. Always the butt of jokes when Web designers congregate, Craigslist looks just as busy and garish as it did in 1995 when Newmark founded it as a Web-based list of his favorite places and activities in the San Francisco Bay Area. The font is frumpy and hard to read. The page layouts have a haphazard look. Lacking images and Javascript, it's as if the site had been frozen at the turn of the new century. It's the anti new media site.

Patrons of Craigslist must appreciate the mess, however, because they are loyal and have not migrated to slicker sites that have tried to top the original. Accidentally or intentionally, Craigslist has grown to be an Internet company with revenues exceeding $150 million, yet it employs only about 30 people. There's simply no way a print newspaper can compete with employee-to-sales ratios like that.

GENIUS OR THE GREAT UNRAVELING?

The worldwide phenomenon called *American Idol* is every bit as slick as Craigslist is plain. From the aerial shots of stadiums filled with eager contestants, to the cringe-worthy auditions, to the stress-filled rehearsal halls, and, finally, to the theatrical grand finale in the Kodak Theater, *American Idol* has made itself the purveyor of a particular kind of American dream: pop stardom. The dream resonates worldwide, too. *American Idol* and its clones are now seen in 100 different nations across the globe. The competition in the United States alone racks up as many votes in a season as Barack Obama received to become president—over 100 million, and remember, that's each season.

In the United States, as elsewhere, *American Idol* has become a cultural touchstone. Day-after watercooler conversations center on the season's favorite contenders, the unfathomable song choices and the so-called pitchiness of various performances, along with the ignominy of landing in the audience's bottom three. And then there's the evil genius whom everyone loves to hate, Simon Cowell. He's the censorious judge whose acid assessments of contestant talent are painfully accurate.

But not everybody appreciates what *American Idol* represents. For many who consider themselves sophisticates, *American Idol* is the program they love to loathe, mostly because it is so outrageously popular and unapologetically populist. For competing TV executives, the antipathy is competition-based, grudging and palpable. They hate it and criticize it, and passionately wish they'd thought of it. From a ratings standpoint, they refer to the show as the Death Star, knowing that programs scheduled against *American Idol* on Tuesday and Wednesday nights are doomed. The big three networks have given up even trying to compete against Fox in those time slots.

Many musicians, too, taste bile at the very mention of *American Idol*. The more serious songwriters and performers around the world consider *American Idol* to be something of a fatal attraction—so enticing, yet so dangerous to one's artistic freedom and future earning power. Every *American*

Idol contestant is required to sign a very restrictive contract that basically gives *American Idol* rights to anything the singer does during or up to three months after the season. Get cut after the first audition? *American Idol* could still own your output for up to a year. Score a hit single after placing third or lower on the show—it has happened—and it's *American Idol* or its parent company, 19 Entertainment, that pockets a significant share of the money. Even well-established artists such as Carrie Underwood and Kelly Clarkson are continuing to pay judge/producer Simon Cowell and his publishing house, Syco, whenever their work is recorded, licensed, or otherwise used. All of which leaves lead singer Chris Martin of the hit band Coldplay genially fuming. Of *American Idol*'s founding producer, Simon Fuller, a smiling Martin has been quoted as saying, "He should be melted down into glue."

But the segment of the music industry most entitled to hate *American Idol* is A&R, or artists and repertoire, the breed of record-company executives who function as talent scouts for the industry. *American Idol* saves its most lethal blow for these star-makers, denying them their longstanding and traditionally unassailable role as gatekeeper of super stardom. Now, instead of clever musicologists with a commercial ear screening the demos and going to the clubs, the teeming masses armed with text-enabled cell phones are calling the shots.

Think of the *American Idol* business model as though it were manufacturing. It's as if you could skip much of your research and development and marketing and simply put your half-baked ideas in front of your prospective buyers. No focus groups, no feasibility studies, no market research—it's all up to consumers themselves to tell you what they'll open their wallets for. No more guessing at how many people might be interested in your product or spending sleepless nights worrying about adoption rates or product acceptance or any of that. As others have averred, *American Idol* gets paid to let the audience figure out what product to produce and then it gets paid for the finished product.

But wait, there's more. There is a web of profit opportunities for Fuller and company that reaches beyond the TV show and music—broadcast rights, syndication, product placement, endorsements, sponsorships, and so on. There is almost nothing related to *American Idol* that 19 Entertainment doesn't profit from and handsomely. The most recent guess at the value of the show and its various revenue streams is $900 million.

Still, you can find plenty of jaded music-industry insiders and observers who don't find what *American Idol* does new or all that shocking. It's been known for decades that everyone along the music-industry food chain is pretty well versed on how to make a buck at the artist's expense. If *American*

Idol is guiltier of cashing in, they say, it's only by degrees. They further reject the notion that somehow *American Idol* is what's killing A&R. A&R has been dying for quite awhile, they argue, as recording labels embattled by music downloads (both legal and illegal) turn away from the search for risky new talent. They've found it safer to bet on artists with a developed fan base and a proven sales record.

Ironically, it's that safety-seeking that really cranks up *Idol* creator Fuller's ire. Asked to diagnose the music industry's woes, he faults record-company executives in general and A&R people specifically. "Don't get me started," he told London's *Sunday Times* in a 2002 profile. "They're so lazy and spoiled. They're mainly interested in ego and money and, worst of all, because they change jobs so often, they have no loyalty to their artists. They've slowly been diminishing the value of artists for years by abusing their back catalogs, releasing endless compilations just to get the numbers to add up."

Fuller fulminates further regarding the music industry's "abysmal decision-making," the best example of which, he says, is letting radio continue to play artists' songs for free. He calls it "giving away the crown jewels." An industry that depends on radio and TV for promotion, that recognizes that radio and TV largely wouldn't exist without music-industry products, and yet gains no revenue from the music or clout over how the music is used—well, no wonder that industry is in decline, Fuller concludes.

He knows what he's talking about because, interestingly enough, Fuller built *American Idol* (or *Pop Idol,* as it began in Great Britain) on his own background in A&R. That's right—Fuller started out as the kind of star-maker he's now putting out of work. As a talent scout for Chrysalis Records, Fuller signed the songwriters that gave Madonna her first hit, "Holiday," in 1984. He took a pass on Madonna herself, it is said, because he just wasn't impressed.

Increasingly disgusted by record executives' greed, stupidity, and sloth, Fuller soon moved to talent management. In 1985 he scored big with an artist named Paul Hardcastle, whose techno-rap, anti–Vietnam War hit, "19," became a worldwide smash. (Figuring 19 must be his lucky number, Fuller named his nascent music empire 19 Entertainment shortly thereafter.) Fuller also managed the Spice Girls for a time, and he still manages Scottish blue-eyed soul singer Annie Lennox.

Nonetheless, even from his earliest days in the business, Fuller was looking far beyond the record-selling prospects of any one artist or stable of artists. As British music executive Lucien Grainge of Universal Music UK has explained it, Fuller was "one of the first people in artist management to treat artists as entertainment brands. He has a real feel for media, TV, and sponsorship. He understands the big picture."

Not surprisingly, none of the established TV networks saw the spark of genius when Fuller's producing partners pitched them *American Idol* in 2001. But newcomer Fox did. Perhaps Fox signed on because the new network was hungry for a fast route to commercial parity with the likes of CBS, NBC, and ABC. Or perhaps it was because Fuller himself took over and made the pitch, promising broad appeal, easy acquisition of sponsors and partnership deals, and, eventually, creation of a global music brand. Whatever the essential combination, it worked. "It was almost like he was pitching a dream," recalls Fox reality-TV executive Mike Darnell on the entertainment Web site *Blender* in 2004. "He mapped the whole thing out, from start to finish," and "[his] vision proved to be uncannily accurate."

It's not at all an overstatement to say that *American Idol* has become the driving force in pop music. Each season of the competition produces a winner and a runner-up, both of whom are immediately very marketable or, more accurately, have already been premarketed. Often, there are one or two more contestants from the top 10 who catch on with the music-buying public as well. What room is there left in the industry for new talent, if *American Idol* winners and contestants have taken over all the real estate? As Peter Robinson, contributing editor of *New Musical Express*, said of Fuller in the *London Evening Standard*, "He is on the brink of setting the agenda for the pop industry around the world." I'd argue that that brink has been well and truly crossed.

WHY SETTLE FOR A BITE WHEN YOU CAN EAT THE WHOLE THING?

Unlike Craig Newmark, it probably can't be said of Steve Jobs that he never dreamed iTunes would transform the music business. He's too prescient not to have foreseen that the dissociation of songs from albums would depress CD sales and set the major recording companies on the path to penury. But the knowledge surely didn't stop him. Like Sherman's March to the Sea, Jobs started at the creative end of the industry and continued his slash-and-burn path through retail.

First, iTunes took on CDs, the cleverest of bundled products, crippling the main vehicle of music labels for delivering music to the buying public. Then the damage spread to stores such as Tower Records, Virgin Music Store, and untold numbers of others, all of which found their businesses decimated by the public's uninterest in CDs. Why pay $16 for a whole CD, buyers properly reasoned, if they could buy their three favorite songs from the CD for 99 cents each?

Today Wal-Mart, Best Buy, Target, and other discounters continue to sell CDs from music floor space that is continually contracting, but there is no longer any national business of scale, nothing bricks-and-mortar, simply nothing in the storefront realm that exists exclusively to sell music. It's all gone. It's been leveled by Apple's appetite for destruction. While at one time all recorded music was sold from a store on a main street somewhere, now close to 40 percent of it comes from a cyber source that could be anywhere.

Jobs's defenders recognize the result, but point out causes that are slightly more complicated. They say that Jobs saw the problem of illegal downloads and believed he could make regular music lovers honest citizens again—if only he could bring music prices down. At 99 cents per song, the price he chose was an outrage to the already-wounded recording industry. Many of the industry's leading labels tried to hold out for a better price, but Jobs simply out-waited them. He knew that with free peer-to-peer downloads extirpating the business models of the record labels, time was on his side.

A FIRE THAT'S WHITE HOT

Will books be the next technology to be destroyed? There's certainly a case to be made that the destruction of the book is not just imminent but well underway—thanks to online retailer Amazon. Its Kindle reader does away with bound paper volumes and puts books, magazines, and other written material on an easy-to-use digital device. Instead of paging through weighty tomes and folding corners to mark your place, you're likely to find your reading future in a slim, lightweight device that always knows your name and never forgets where you left off. Barnes & Noble with the Nook, Sony with its Reader, and now Apple with its iPad all want a piece of the action.

Bibliophiles are horrified. What about the satisfying heft of holding a book? What about the musty smell of pages tested by time and turned by many readers—or just by you? What about the beauty of the bookshelf, with its march of titles, sizes, and colors, each combination giving clues to the character of what lies between the covers? Kill the book, kill the culture, Amazon's critics say.

Amazon CEO Jeff Bezos doesn't think so. Without a trace of sentimentality, he describes the book as we've known it since the age of Gutenberg and the invention of movable type as just another obsolete distribution tool waiting to be destroyed by a new and improved model.

"It's important to embrace new technologies instead of [fighting] them," Bezos asserted in a 2007 interview with PBS talk show host Charlie Rose. "You know, people forget that the book itself is a technology. It evolved from clay tablets to parchment to paper. We humans co-evolve with our tools. We change our tools, and then our tools change us."

At around $200, the Kindle requires a significant investment on the part of the consumer. But there's value in its many features. Nearly any book you want to download and read costs a mere $9.99—instead of the $25 or $30 charged in a bookstore. You can browse the first chapter of any book for free, just to ensure it's something you want to read. There's a search function allowing you to look for names, topics, locations, and other curiosities. You can click on a word and have it defined for you by a 250,000-word internal dictionary, or learn more about a topic by calling up any of 45 million Wikipedia pages. You can make notes in margins, highlight passages, and underline words. When you're done with a book you can delete it. But if you want to reread it you can download it for free—and your notations will still be there, just as if you'd put the book on your shelf.

While Bezos clearly doesn't waste any tears over the shelving of books as information-delivery devices, he does profess to care deeply about the future of reading. In fact, Bezos says his devotion to long-form reading is the main motivator behind his company's introduction of the Kindle. Some forms of learning occur only by stepping into a character's shoes, he says, or by considering a point of view as seen through the author's eyes. Society will be the poorer, Bezos believes, if long-form reading falls victim to information snacking.

But won't all of this actually threaten reading itself? The data suggests it's already happening. Some 411,000 new titles were published in America in 2008, and more than 3 billion books were sold in the United States. Growth in the mainstay market of fiction and nonfiction for adult readers was a mere 4.3 percent. As is the case in most Western industrialized countries, leisure reading in America is down, especially among the young. The share of the entertainment dollar in books is also down, by seven percent since 1985.

But Bezos doesn't consider these stats as an indictment of reading as a pastime. Rather, he thinks the book market has been lagging because customers are awaiting new technology, a 2.0 version of the bound volume with better features and mobility. While holding out for the new-and-improved, they've been information-snacking like crazy but not necessarily enjoying it. Bezos explained to Charlie Rose, "I value my BlackBerry—I'm convinced it makes me more productive—but I don't want to read a three-hundred-page document on it. Nor do I want to read something hundreds of pages long on my desktop computer or my laptop. People do more of whatever's convenient and friction-free."

Bezos sees no conflict between his self-acknowledged "missionary" zeal for reading and his concomitant determination to make paper-and-glue books obsolete. But others do. Publishers have signed on kicking and screaming, especially around the issue of pricing. Clearly, their enthusiasm for anything that promotes the work of authors has been dampened by the growing fear that they are witnessing the end of publishing as they've known it since 1430.

Bezos attempts to soothe by predicting that eReaders will hasten a renaissance in the printed word. New and beneficial things are coming, he promises, and publishers may stand to benefit not only from things too new to be imagined but also from some Kindle-inspired variations on old and forgotten themes. For example, what's to stop the Kindle from reviving Charles Dickens-style serialization, the telling of stories in installments? Moreover, what prevents a future author from engaging in a cyber-dialog with readers on plot and character development as he or she writes, with the Kindle as a go-between? Surveying the future landscape from his vantage point, Bezos concluded his Kindle remarks on Charlie Rose's show by saying, "It just doesn't make sense to me that printing our books on dead trees is the final step in the evolution of books."

Amazon is putting plenty of bucks behind Bezos' homiletic assertion. In fact, the story goes that a Kindle-project employee once asked Bezos how much he was prepared to spend on developing and marketing the reader. In his 2008 interview with *Business Week*'s Peter Burrows, Bezos quotes himself as retorting, "How much do we have?"

You could interpret that quip as Bezos fighting for the future of books. But there is another way to look at it—and it leads us right back to why Amazon is a transformative company. Quite simply, the Kindle completes the destruction that Bezos has such an appetite for. It's the last step in his relentless march toward a vertically integrated book industry.

Via Amazon, Bezos has made it possible for customers to tap into an almost limitless source of books, find a desired book, search its pages to ensure it's what they want, check competitors' prices, consider whether to buy it used or new, and with one click, make the purchase. What's more, thanks to some pretty savvy algorithms, they can receive uncannily accurate recommendations on other books they might like and even maintain their own onsite wish list of future purchases.

No wonder Amazon, a $15-billion company, controls 6 percent of the $136 billion online retail market. No surprise, either, that it sells up to 30 percent of the books purchased in the United States and, if we remove actual stores from the calculation, that it's the site of choice for nearly four-fifths of online book buyers. Creative destruction indeed.

LOVE AND DEATH

What I find most interesting in these exemplars of transformation through destruction is, for want of a better term, the *affection* displayed. All of the founders we've talked about display something akin to love for their products and services. They aren't out simply to dynamite a path to success for themselves, or to destroy competition for the sake of racking up points or amassing street cred. They're after something more—much more.

We can argue with these innovators about what their real motivations are, but if we take them at their word, theirs is at least a strong conviction that the world has been waiting for their solution—and really, really needs it. With a belief that strong, you'll knock over existing players almost unconsciously and unsentimentally. An appetite for destruction is something that isn't born or bred, then—it's an autonomic response, a reflex. The founders of Craigslist, Apple, and Amazon see themselves as nothing more or less than committed problem solvers. And their customers are merely folks who perhaps didn't realize they had a problem until offered its solution.

There is something else that catalyzes an appetite for destruction: an almost compulsive desire to eliminate or replace the gatekeepers. Underlying many of the stories in this chapter is a healthy disdain for the existing order. Why should certain people decide which music should be popular? Why should recording companies get to determine what songs need to be sold together on a single CD? Why does somebody need to book an ad with the local newspaper to sell a used car?

You could call it corporate democratization, perhaps. Simon Fuller wants to do a better job than the talent scouts of bringing music to the masses, and Jeff Bezos wants to ensure that you can get the books you want when you want them, by giving you the means to carry a digital book shelf in your hand. As these examples have shown, the consumer stands to benefit in astounding ways by virtue of these corporate marauders. Remember Jarvis's earlier quote about efficiency. However, if you have the misfortune of being an incumbent competitor in a market such as these, it's probably time to begin the self-examination and reinvention we will explore in the remaining two chapters.

Chapter 8

DETACHMENT

At the center of the Shiva image is the very depiction of calm at the center of the storm. While arms whirl and legs beat out the rhythm of life, the face is a relaxed mask. It is as if Shiva has found a way to be *detached* from the action at the fringes while participating in the things that matter. Like Shiva, transformative companies manage to remain objective, find fresh perspective, and calm their noisy worlds. They evaluate themselves frequently and consistently ask themselves the most revelatory questions.

It was during one of his Think Week breaks, which Bill Gates holds twice annually, that the Microsoft CEO fully recognized the Internet's existential threat to his software business. Having silenced the daily chatter of e-mails and meetings for seven full days, he was able to sit and evaluate reams of reading material—much of it provided by his own employees. Gates came back from the short exile in 1995 with a detailed message to his Microsoft management titled "The Internet Tidal Wave." It was a strategy for remaining not just viable but meaningful in a new age. Had the memo not become part of the evidence in *U.S. v. Microsoft*, the monumental antitrust case, we might never have known the extent to which Gates's Think Week influenced the future fortunes of Microsoft and its competitors—for both good and ill.

Amazon founder Jeff Bezos uses his periodic disappearances—a few days or a week anonymously hoisting boxes in a fulfillment center or holed up in a hotel room—to reconfirm the basic mission of his company and commit to new initiatives such as the now-popular Kindle reader. "It's always Day One," the cheerful titan has been known to say. In fact, the phrase is the centerpiece of his personal credo as he described it in a videotaped speech titled "Everything I Know." To him it means it's always the right time to start fresh. Could it be that Bezos's well-known confidence and optimism, along with his consistent ability to convert tactical miscues into long-term strategic wins, all stem from the time he schedules for observation and internal conversation?

Experience confirms that at the heart of many a transformative company's success you will find a steadfast commitment to *detachment*. It's a term I use to describe the periodic pauses companies and their leaders take to step outside of themselves, adopt a critical view of their enterprise and the market, and, if need be, make course corrections. In this chapter we will consider some of the ways in which companies step out of the daily grind so as to stimulate creative self-examination, initiate problem solving, and plan for strategic change. What we'll see through various examples is that while the original impetus for detached reflection often comes from a visionary CEO, the practice achieves its greatest power when it reaches down and outward to include others.

WHY DETACH AND REFLECT?

A bias for action. A focus on execution. Much of the published guidance available to businesses today focuses on relentlessly moving forward. Honeywell's CEO, Larry Bossidy, even wrote a bestseller called *Execution, the Discipline of Getting Things Done*. Meanwhile, the tools offered for strategic planning—whether it's SWOT (strengths, weaknesses, opportunities, and threats) analysis or blue ocean strategy—are merely a subset of the desired outcome, which is action. Too often the tools are used without much consideration, and the process becomes reactionary instead of proactive. Deliberation is for wimps, the pundits seem to infer. Do not hesitate.

Such advice undoubtedly has its place. But a close examination of transformative companies reveals the merit of having a bias for *proactive inaction* for at least long enough to consider, in an integrative way, what could and should be done. Gates was certainly looking at what should be done, and, indeed, plenty of detached reflection is used solely for spotting and addressing problems. For me, however, the real value in the process relates to the second part, what could be done. Looking laterally, scanning for possibilities, gathering data, forming impressions: all of these have great and largely unappreciated value for the business seeking a creative view of the future and each has influenced the success of the transformative companies we've studied.

What frequently surfaces from these reflective periods of inactivity is first a separation and then synthesis and integration of the multitude of factors influencing a business—things that normally blend together into a single protean blob during our chockablock days. I'm reminded of a quote attributed to iconic rock promoter Billy Graham about the Grateful Dead. He said the Grateful Dead were not the best at what they did; rather, they were the only ones who did what they did. When you think about transformative enterprises, you realize that most have found ways of integrating things that other people hadn't thought of integrating. They have created something new, something fresh, and very occasionally, something that taps into the universal.

I think about integration a great deal as I evaluate portfolio companies. I look for inspired connections and associations that lead to ingenious business concepts, because, unless you are integrating elements that come from places that initially seem to be disconnected, it's very hard to be transformative. You may be the best at whatever your business does, but it's almost impossible to consider new horizons if you haven't given yourself a chance to find them. Unfortunately, too few businesses allow themselves that sort of opportunity.

Remember that it was Bezos of Amazon who thought of book selling as essentially a logistics issue. Since America has one of the best logistics and distribution systems in the world, it's been only logical for manufacturers to employ a just-in-time inventory system. To apply the same thinking to book selling, to compress that retail experience into the mold of a manufacturing distribution system—now, that's integrative thinking. To complete his long-envisioned seamless connection between book content and customer, Bezos went well beyond his company's core competency to develop the Kindle reader. Why has it taken Barnes and Noble three generations of Kindles to introduce the Nook? I suspect it's not because they couldn't find someone to build the hardware. More likely, they were unable to put the conceptual pieces together. Bezos took the lead because he is an integrative thinker, well-known for his ability to put himself in situations that allow for detached reflection.

Gates is something of a different story. His lack of prevision that Netscape represented the tip of an ominous iceberg seems ridiculous in hindsight, as Netscape founder Marc Andreessen's mug was staring at Gates from just about every magazine cover. Gates's Think Week recognition of the elemental threat posed by this upstart and those coming in its wake was just barely timely, but it did happen. His annual seven-day sojourn gave him the quietism at last to see the danger and formulate a plan to counter it. Much is changing at Microsoft since Gates's retirement, but Think Week is something that his successors say they are trying to continue.

DETACHMENT FOR PROBLEM SOLVING

Bill Gates used that critical Think Week to solve a problem—one that he hadn't known existed, or hadn't fully appreciated. More CEOs should learn from his near-miss experience. Fast-growth companies, in particular, benefit when the CEO is able to anticipate problems and make periodic adjustments in both tactics and strategy. A one-week-a-year sabbatical à la Gates is a good idea, but something more continual is better.

One CEO who makes an ongoing practice of detached reflection is Michael Chasen of Blackboard, who told me it has grown to be a significant part of his job description. After more than 10 years in educational information technology, he finds that there is a continual parade loop of things that go wrong or no longer work—mostly as a consequence of growth.

"There were two of us when we started and now we have 1,200 employees. That means you're doing a reorganization every twelve to eighteen months, just to adjust. As you get bigger it's hard to make the transitions, but as painful as it is, you have to try to stay nimble." Chasen pointedly told me that, like any fast-growth company, Blackboard isn't just a train going down the tracks; it's a train building the tracks as it travels them. "You can't wait and make changes ninety degrees at a time. To keep the tracks straight, you need to be constantly adjusting. I look at things at least monthly and, while it may add up to a ninety-degree change, it's never more than two or three degrees at a time."

In the interview that produced these comments, Chasen mentioned that he hasn't felt the need to delegate or institutionalize the role of change agent. He's assumed the role comfortably, without thinking too much about it. "It's just inherent in every day for me now. If there's a list of 100 problems, I just keep cycling through them. Big problems become small problems or go away, only to return again." How does he maintain such a strategic focus on a continuing basis? "It's the legacy of having a Jewish mother," Chasen quips. "Never being satisfied."

Netflix is a clear example of a company that works to include many of its employees in its efforts to achieve a detached perspective amid a ferociously competitive market. The company conducts a quarterly business review, like many companies do, but "this is not an easy offsite," as marketing executive Steve Swasey said on the company Web site several years ago. "Everybody comes with their best work and their biggest mistakes, and we super-analyze . . . the good and the bad, and the ugly. We look at the smallest detail with excruciating attention so that we can continue to improve the business, which of course lowers cost, [and] drives greater efficiency and higher customer satisfaction." (Netflix's customer satisfaction numbers are consistently the highest in the video business.) Swasey says that there are two key questions driving Netflix's version of detached reflection, stated or unstated, namely: is this what the corporation exists to do and is this best for the company and its objectives?

Netflix has been known to say of itself, "We are not process-intensive. What we are is progress-intensive." Another company that could make the same claim is Cognizant Technologies Inc., where it's almost easier to identify when detached reflection is not occurring. It's that ongoing.

THE CONTINUAL CONSIDERATION
OF WHAT'S NEXT

A few years ago a big-name management consultant blew into a customer-oriented conference held by Cognizant Technologies Inc., the information-technology outsourcing firm. However, he did not blow back out again after his speech, as marquee consultants often do. He stayed for lunch, and then he stayed for the afternoon, too. To the surprise of all, the consultant was still mingling and observing through dinner and Casino Night. Finally he came to board chairman John Klein looking perplexed. "I can't understand this company," he said. "Of all the companies I've been to, something is very, very different about this one. Something's going on here."

There's a lot going on at Cognizant. We explored some of it in Chapter 4, the process chapter, but I think it's likely that this not-to-be-named consultant picked up on the unusual nature of the customer-employee relationships that were on display at the conference. Cognizant, you see, is uncommonly committed to a version of detached reflection that requires both the company and its customers to stop, collect data, hold discussions, and deeply consider where things are going—not just for Cognizant, but for its customers, too. Involving customers in the planning process and making true partners of them is likely at the heart of the uncharacteristically collaborative relationship that the consultant could sense at the conference but couldn't quite identify.

CEO Frank D'Souza has trouble putting this actively reposed relationship into words, too. "It's just something in our DNA," he told me. "When people tell me that there's something different about us, I always ask them to describe it, because we really don't know." Typically he hears about intangibles like corporate culture and employee attitude. But neither they nor D'Souza are certain that any such words suffice.

I believe that part of what impresses people about Cognizant is the sangfroid it displays at its center. That stillness comes, paradoxically, from a continuing churn of transformative strategic planning together with Cognizant's customers. In my conversation with him, D'Souza seemed to confirm this view: calm on the surface, dancing blissfully amid the flames.

From its earliest days, Cognizant made energetic use of planning and training to establish a hierarchically flat, virtual company where employees could make their own decisions on behalf of clients. D'Souza and other leaders knew that this was truly the only way for Cognizant to operate out of New Jersey while maintaining most of its knowledge workforce in India and its clients worldwide. However, it has always required careful monitoring of what D'Souza calls "inflection points" to ensure that the company's capabilities keep up with its decentralized growth. The inflection points are looked for on the horizon by multiple ranks within the organization so that when they appear, both the company and its customers are ready. Whenever such a vatic point is recognized, key employees meet both together and with customers to ensure that Cognizant continues to address the market's needs.

I asked D'Souza to explain. "In terms of planning," he replied, "we ask each business leader and functional leader to prepare not just for this year or the next. We ask them, 'What are you going to be doing in the next three or four years?'" A critical part of each exercise is to project future inflection points. These points reveal themselves as the company grows and can affect anything—the technological infrastructure, the business-process infrastructure, or the management and leadership layer. "They are the points beyond which the ways of doing things as you'd done them in the past don't scale," explains D'Souza.

"In a company that grows at a more modest pace, these inflection points happen less frequently and perhaps more predictably," D'Souza continues. "What we have found is that, because of our hyper-growth, they happen more frequently and often simultaneously with one another. Every year we consciously look at this and think, 'What will be the inflection points we expect to hit in the next one to two years, what are the key bottlenecks to our growth, and how do we address [them]?' We try to take action ahead of the curve to be sure that we are not creating internal constraints to our own growth as we go forward."

Cognizant asks its customers similar questions. Where is their business headed? What will they be doing in three to five years, and, given that future direction, what will they need in outsourced information technology to support this direction? Cognizant takes pains to ensure that customers do not limit their responses to things that the company currently knows how to do. As board chairman Klein explained in my interview with him and D'Souza, "What they tell us gives us good food for thought as to what things are on their radar screen. We take that input, combine it with industry studies and expert opinions on trends, and then say, 'What does this mean for us?'" The internal debate that follows plots Cognizant's future. "We separate the me-toos from the things in which we think we could reasonably achieve dominance, establish six or eight priorities, and then take updates throughout the year from the task forces assigned to working on them," says Klein.

As a venture capitalist who hears "We're too busy to plan" far too frequently from some of the emerging companies in my portfolio, I find Cognizant inspiring. It's always a monumental challenge to find the time and the energy for a strategic planning exercise, but the best CEOs remain disciplined about doing it. And when for some reason they can't, it leaves these high-performers profoundly uneasy. Phil Wiser, the founder-CEO of Sezmi, has grown accustomed to devoting at least a full day each quarter to planning—and remember, as of this writing, his is a company with zero revenues. When the planning rhythm collapsed in the year prior to the introduction of Sezmi's products, it made Wiser nervous. He told me, "We've gotten to September of 2009 and I don't know what 2010 looks like. It's really disconcerting. Usually I know by fall what our goals are."

Really good companies, especially the transformative ones, welcome the opportunity to detach and reflect, and miss it when it's gone on too long. Can any company make a ritual of this? Probably, but Frank D'Souza of Cognizant is convinced that it's a more effective discipline when born with the company. "We grew up this way, so we don't think anything of it. But it would be difficult for a traditional company to change itself to operate the way we operate." D'Souza believes that his inflection-point exercises are made more successful by the democratized nature of his organization, one in which middle managers run their own profit-and-loss statements almost as if they were separate businesses. "We [take] comfort in letting people make decisions because we have trained them in what we think is important. In a traditional company, they would have nightmares trying to change to that level of being a flat organization with so much delegated responsibility."

What D'Souza says is undoubtedly true. Detached reflection does seem to occur more readily where there are knowledge workers who thrive in near autonomy. For example, companies in pharmaceuticals and allied fields tend to consider detached reflection as something of a built-in, because companies such as Genentech and AstraZeneca maintain a quasi-academic environment in which each idea is put through a peer-review process. The atmosphere in such companies is all about gathering data, and making and testing hypotheses. It's integrative, and it can't help but involve detached reflection.

Another example of a company that maintains an environment conducive to detached reflection is the highly transformative Google, known for its 20 percent time. It's a concept that 3M pioneered decades ago and credited with the inventions of Scotch tape and Post-It notes, though the percentage back then was 15 percent instead of 20. Google engineers are encouraged to spend the equivalent of one day each week working on some sort of pet project, something that their normal activities would prevent them from exploring. In the pursuit of great new concepts—which have included Google News, Gmail, Orkut, Google Sky, and Google Grants—these employees are doing what's essential to the productive use of detached reflection. They're taking the outsider's point of view to determine where Google's next opportunities lie. In so doing, they're integrating their own knowledge and interests with whatever influences may have crossed their desks or minds. Other fans of the activity, to name just two, include Facebook with its Hackathons, where programmers clean cobwebs out of existing features and pave the way for developing new ones, and Atlassian, an Australian software firm that encourages its employees to develop new applications for its products in marathon bursts called FedEx days—because, originally, the deliverables were due overnight. You can argue whether the intent is detached reflection or not, but the results just as effective.

FINDING CREATIVE CALM

In a technology, entertainment, and design (TED) talk titled "The Power of Time Off" given by Stefan Sagmeister, the New York City designer declares that all the work he did over seven full years is due to the one year he closed his business and took a sabbatical. For him, the products of a prolonged sort of detached reflection were quite robust. It was a time that put him in touch with new influences and ideas, ones he couldn't have encountered without having left Manhattan for Bali.

Few of us can manage that sort of a break mid-career, but we can perhaps provide ourselves a bit of respite, a few moments each day to, as they say, "calm the ripples on the pond to see more clearly." Meditation is very old and very Eastern, but it's rapidly becoming one of the newest and most favored methods of stimulating detached reflection in corporate America. During his talk, Sagmeister mentions that his sabbatical was enhanced by one particular discipline he adopted during that time: ritualized meditation.

Amid the likes of Apple, Google, and AstraZeneca, there is a growing cohort of highly successful companies that are offering employees the means to learn meditation and the time to practice it. With the help of consultants—sometimes tennis-ball-equipped to illustrate how to "drop into the moment"—employees are discovering the calm and the creativity that are associated with turning inward. Google says it enhances the "emotional intelligence" of its employees. AstraZeneca has used it during breaks in day-long business retreats to give employees another choice besides zoning out or bingeing on sugar or caffeine to stay alert.

Regular practitioners of meditation report a variety of benefits, many of which are backed up by research. Laboratories at the National Institutes of Health, the University of Massachusetts, and the Mind/Body Medical Institute at Harvard have reported that meditation increases brain wave activity, reduces stress, improves intuition, and boosts concentration. Yet another study, this one using an admittedly small sample of just 12 Buddhist monks recommended by the Dalai Lama, produced neurological findings suggesting that meditation changes brain waves in ways that are associated with a greater capacity for focused thought.

Now, even today, in our globalized era, it might seem odd to Western ears to hear that meditation will be a featured activity during a corporate offsite. But we must remember that meditation is as disciplined a practice as any quarterly strategic-planning session and a lot less dangerous than a ropes course. To be good at it requires practice and commitment, and many of us find it requires more effort than we are willing to put into it. This is particularly true in the West, where we're always looking for the straight line to an outcome. Meditation seldom produces one. Therefore, the companies that are making use of meditation recognize that neither corporation nor individual can expect to see an immediately recognizable benefit—*and that it is still worth doing*. That's because a mind that has been stilled and opened is a mind that is prepared for integrative thinking and new possibilities.

Networking consultant Keith Ferrazzi (author of *Never Eat Alone*, 2005) attributes his current career to Vipassana meditation, among other things. The practice requires 10-day stints of meditation cut off from the outside world, an isolation that Ferrazzi imposes on himself annually while continuing to meditate daily on his own. The beauty of Vipassana, he and other practitioners say, is its ability to help one *see things as they are*. Other forms of meditation exist, but clarity of vision is a common pursuit of the various strands. In fact, one meditation consultant, Australian Stephen Manallack, argues that this is its most beneficial aspect for business leaders. In an online article posted in the summer of 2009, he writes:

> Danger lurks in many seemingly harmless parts of your organization, and this danger can be best described as the acceptance of bad habits. Once bad habits creep in, if you are not a watchful leader, these habits are passed on to others and gradually become part of your corporate culture. Failure is just around the corner.
>
> Spotting bad habits sounds easy but is hard to do—most leaders exist in a kind of cocoon, surrounded by myths and a denial of what is true. Denial among those at the top, and around the top, is endemic.

Meditation, Manallack says, helps leaders "break out of the 'cocoon of denial.'"

My own regular meditation involves spending lots of time staring out the window doing what used to be called daydreaming, or going for a long trail run. This is especially true when I'm about to begin raising a fund that will deploy a significant amount of capital for the ensuing three to five years.

In such periods, I also notice that I gravitate to things that broaden my horizons—photography, art, and other influences that tend to be cross-cultural or interdisciplinary. When I'm looking for where the next spurt of growth is likely to come from, I find that I can't get there from reading three articles in *Forbes*. I need to get myself into a state of creative contemplation, and, for me, it begins with looking out the window and soaking up new images and ideas.

Others disengage by going outside of their comfort zone. My friend Verne Harnish, in his book *Mastering the Rockefeller Habits*, reports that he gains his detached reflection by periodically attending a conference in an unfamiliar industry. Being kinetic about it is fine, I think; you don't have to subscribe to anybody's idea of detached reflection but your own. If deep breathing or sitting in a sweat lodge is your thing, great. If noodling over a checklist floats your boat, also great. The method for achieving detached reflection matters far less than the outcome, which ought to be a more integrated view of where opportunity lies and where vulnerabilities exist. Find what works, make the time, and just do it.

Still not convinced? Need a cautionary tale to spur you and your company to implement a regimen that involves some sort of detached reflection? Google the story of the Peanut Butter Manifesto, if you're not familiar with it. The leaked internal screed against Yahoo! written by then-marketing executive Brad Garlinghouse is a veritable bill of particulars against a company that had allowed itself to grow without sufficient self-examination. In the memo, Garlinghouse describes a lack of accountability across the various business units of Yahoo!, a proliferation of do-little management, and, most of all, corporate inability to focus energies and investment.

"I've heard our strategy described as spreading peanut butter across the myriad opportunities that continue to evolve in the online world," wrote Garlinghouse. "The result: a thin layer of investment spread across everything we do and thus we focus on nothing in particular." He concludes: "I hate peanut butter." By the time his words hit the newspapers and blogs, his embarrassed bosses—who would have rather heard this discussed in a far smaller venue—were ready to consider the message of this chapter a missed opportunity. Instead, they moved on to what often follows detached reflection: reinvention.

Chapter 9

REINVENTION

Many cultures, including that of Hindus, use serpents to symbolize reincarnation, the constant and eternal quest for self-improvement. The cobra worn like a garland in the Shiva image sheds its skin, suggesting renewal and—in business terms—*reinvention*. Companies that are able to shed old skin and bring into being something new are transformative companies, in the best sense of the word.

In 2006, the term "hot laptop" gained a whole new meaning when a surprising number of laptop computer users were reporting burned fingers from overheated machines, and a few said their machines got so hot that the cases actually glowed red. However, the capper was a photo flashed around the world via the Internet depicting a Dell laptop aflame at a business conference in Japan, as stunned bystanders looked on.

The spate of overheating turned out to be caused by faulty lithium-ion batteries, many of which were eventually recalled by Sony. Though the problem affected most laptop makers, it became associated with Dell's laptops, due primarily to the viral spread of that Japanese photo. Dell accepted its share of responsibility. While other manufacturers laid low during the initial publicity, Dell was quickly out front, talking directly to consumers through a relatively new blog established solely to solicit and receive customer feedback, Direct2Dell.com.

Dell hadn't always been so transparent. In fact, Dell had been through a different sort of baptism by fire about a year earlier, one that had prompted a wholesale reinvention of how it did business with its customers. The catalyst was a 2005 anti-Dell blog swarm that became known as Dell Hell. Spawned by Jeff Jarvis, a blogger who considered his Dell laptop a lemon, the cannonade resulted in a variety of I-hate-Dell Web sites filled with stories of unaddressed customer complaints.

Dell recognized this as the crisis that it was and took action. A company blogger was named. The Direct2Dell Web site was established to open a line of communication between Dell and its customers. Moreover, to make full use of the customer input that began pouring in, Dell established IdeaStorm, a Web site where customers could actually rate and discuss Dell's newest product ideas. Dell saw its negative comments online go from about 50 percent to 23 percent in just a year. In the same period, customers offered 8,000 suggestions, voted on them 600,000 times, and left 64,000 comments. Indeed, so successful was Dell's reinvention that it became a leading case study, touching on topics that remain current today: crowd sourcing and corporate use of social media, to name just two.

Corporations that possess the self-awareness, the willingness, and the wherewithal to reinvent themselves are perhaps the epitome of the transformative-company concepts I've tried to illustrate in this book. They are the ones who not only hold out the promise of being *built for change* but actually demonstrate it. They live it.

There are basically two ways that companies come to a decision to reinvent their products, services, and ways of doing business. One is via the sudden recognition of a problem or a market shift that threatens viability, which certainly describes the reality that was Dell Hell. For an extreme version of the type, you might even hearken back decades to the infamous Johnson & Johnson crisis as it scrambled to repackage products in the wake of the Tylenol poisonings. Such crises demand immediate and often revolutionary change, mobilizing employee buy-in almost overnight. In fact, so galvanizing is the crisis-born reinvention that it's not unheard of for managements at least to consider *creating* a crisis to stimulate change, the downside risk, of course, being the possibility of employees figuring out they've been had.

But there also exists a more evolutionary form of reinvention, one that comes from the disciplined application of detached reflection (as described in the previous chapter.) It's harder to pull off, because it requires a company to put aside things like denial and nostalgia in order to face circumstances as they are. It also forces management to take steps to earn employee support for change that may result in new duties or lost jobs. This kind of change often takes place over years, not months. When done right, the longer-term effort tends to be less traumatic and have stronger staying power. Nonetheless, it requires uncommon commitment on the part of both management and its workforce.

This chapter celebrates reinvention in all its forms and motivations. The hows and whys of reinvention are interesting, but they aren't really the point. What is worthy of recognition is the mere fact that these companies are capable of reinvention—that they have it within their genetic makeup to change. That's rare. Most corporations, like the people who inhabit them, are wedded to what they are already doing. Change comes hard if it comes at all. In my opinion, any attempt at reinvention is heroic.

MOVING WITH THE MARKET

To some extent, companies take measure of their prospects all the time. We hear weekly if not daily of companies shifting, redesigning, reintroducing, and rebranding with the goal of better addressing the market. Radio Shack becomes The Shack. Starbucks introduces instant coffee and, in grocery-store freezers, ice cream. Noting a drop-off in overnight shipping traffic, Fred Smith's company establishes FedEx Ground and begins delivering merchandise instead of documents. But are these examples of reinvention or of something that falls well short of it? I think that true reinvention is a bit like the late Supreme Court Justice Potter Stewart's definition of pornography: "I know it when I see it." I look at the genesis of the supposed reinvention, because it can be telling. More especially, I scan for signs of detachment, the ability—the discipline—to see the market through new eyes.

Hilti Corp. is a highly respected tools manufacturer based in the nation of Liechtenstein. At more than 50 years old, it certainly qualifies as venerable, successful, and perhaps even staid. Yet in the past few years it has managed to readdress its market in a way that is nothing short of reinvention.

Having recognized that tool purchases and maintenance have become an expense that leaves contractors cash-strapped, Hilti created Fleet Management, whereby customers pay a monthly fee to rent tools instead of buying them. The arrangement—largely unknown in tool-manufacturing circles—assures contractors of predictable costs and access to all tools necessary for their needs. However, the contract, which can run up to five years, does much more than that. Hilti Fleet Management covers all repairs and replacement, provides onsite service, promises unlimited battery exchanges, and adds three sweeteners: personalized labeling, online tracking, and insurance, all of which are designed to deter theft.

Hilti's reinvention was a response to the worldwide economic downturn. Tool sales had slowed, prompting internal discussion of restructuring the company's manufacturing, sales, and service model. There was another factor at work, too. Producers of low-end tools, Hilti's competitors, were gaining market share as credit tightened and construction-industry growth declined.

Taking an outsider's view of their business, Hilti managers recognized that *contractors make money by finishing jobs, not by owning tools.* As the old dictum goes, people don't need drills, they need holes. Hilti sought to adjust its customer value proposition by freeing contractors to focus on quality and efficiency in fulfilling their engagements instead of the buying and maintaining of tools. It was clear from the earliest discussions that switching to a service-oriented business model would require plenty of internal retooling: developing a new profit formula, taking what used to be customer assets back onto Hilti's own balance sheet, establishing warehousing and inventory management, and much more. The biggest task was retraining salespeople to sell a program instead of a product, which is a longer-term process that involves not just craftspeople but CFOs.

Hilti embarked upon Fleet Management believing that the new approach held the best hope of maintaining market share and keeping their customers in business. Certainly the model gave customers an economic reason at least to consider sticking with the high-end producer. Hilti itself estimates that contractors save 30 to 50 percent on their tool costs by switching to Fleet Management contracts. It's "the biggest innovation from Hilti in the last twenty years," says the company's spokesman.

All the time, we see manufacturers, regardless of the industry, respond to the same set of circumstances Hilti faced—cash-strapped customers and low-cost competition. But while others may opt to create a cheaper alternative, perhaps a new line of more affordable products, Hilti is one of the rare ones that choose to reinvent everything. The company looked at its business in a detached way, saw a better way of serving customers, and then initiated organization-wide change to make the reinvention successful.

WHEN THE PAST IS NO LONGER PROLOGUE

It would seem obvious that another spur to reinvention is corporate maturation. As companies grow from startup to emerging company to maturity, they find that the internal structures that once sufficed no longer fit the bill. Yet it's often difficult to change ways of doing business, especially when the changes may alter things that employees have come to consider integral to who they are. The companies that are able to detach and recognize the need for change and then go ahead and make the change are eminently worthy of being called transformative.

The founding cornerstone of the culture at Intuit, makers of Quicken, QuickBooks, and other financial software, was consensus—everybody was part of the decision making. But consensus doesn't scale. When, as early as 1993, middle managers began complaining of needing five sign-offs from the executive suite to hire an assistant, and executives themselves noted ever more incidents in which top-team disagreements slowed progress, founder-CEO Scott Cook began to move toward change, starting with a visioning process. In *Inside Intuit*, a book that goes deep into company history through the eyes of people who lived it, authors Suzanne Taylor and Kathy Schroeder quote from Cook's explanatory memo:

> Often, as companies grow larger, it becomes increasingly difficult to keep growing at a rapid pace, to maintain communications between departments, and to keep focused on a common goal. Rifts can develop, different departments can develop different value systems, and goals can become decentralized. This type of breakdown has led to the demise of many companies today.

With that, Cook took the first steps in what would become a seven-year journey toward reinvention. It included a change from the functionally organized structure Intuit had long favored, to one consisting of business units. It resulted in the closing of underperforming call centers and manufacturing sites, even as the company began investing in, and gearing up for, an Internet-based future. The path wound through three CEOs, each in his own way determined to move the company to a fully managed rigor that was more fitting of a public company about to cross the billion-dollar threshold. Through it all, however, the constant was founder Cook, who represented the human bridge between Intuit's past and its future. He served as both cheerleader and chief critic as the reinvention proceeded.

The biggest changes arrived in 2000 with the hiring of former General Electric executive Steve Bennett. A proud disciple of Jack Welch, Bennett began by stripping away layers of Intuit management that had insulated the company from its customers. "If you have seven sweaters on you don't know the real temperature," the quotable Bennett explained at the time. He instituted a culture that encouraged the questioning of assumptions. According to authors Taylor and Schroeder, this was upsetting to some in the company and invigorating to others. Bennett installed leadership training designed to flush out the last residue of the old consensus ethic at Intuit and prod managers to take charge. When critics predicted a negative impact on innovation, Bennett disagreed. In *Inside Intuit*, he was quoted as saying, "Ideas without operational rigor just fall apart." Soon, employees who knew of operational deficiencies began to name them, no longer fearing ostracism. With Bennett's eventual introduction of Six Sigma process improvements, Intuit began to see reductions of 40 percent in some cost centers and up to 70 percent in others. Bennett was, as one manager put it, "methodical [and] straightforward—but revolutionary."

The most important and potentially fractious change that Bennett engendered had to do with focus. A company that had always kept its eyes unblinkingly trained on the customer, Intuit would now widen its view and devote as much attention to shareholders. In other words, it would think as much about making money as it did about serving the customer. This was not a shift that was universally welcomed. Nor was it greeted happily by all when Bennett changed the performance evaluation system and began giving the biggest salary bumps to the people making the greatest difference in Intuit's prospects. But this is where Cook's presence and support made such a difference. In companies where the founder is gone or is a reluctant convert to restructuring, what often results is an atmosphere of foisted change—the kind that most humans reflexively avoid. But with the founder on hand and fully invested in finding the company's next phase, disruptive changes rise to the level of inspired reinvention.

REINVENTION IN REDMOND

For a contrasting tale to Intuit's in the area of mature reinvention, we need look no further than what's being attempted at Microsoft. Just as Bill Gates earned the company another full decade of relevancy and profits by refocusing on the Internet, a recognized software genius named Ray Ozzie is laboring mightily to connect Redmond, Washington, to the Internet (i.e., Cloud) instead of a desktop, and adjust it to a world where customers are offered subscriptions instead of boxed software.

The chattering class isn't giving Ozzie much time or patience in pursuit of these goals. The first blog entries predicting Ozzie's departure or failure (or both) began appearing no less than six months after he was given the reins. They talked of how Microsoft's siloed culture had been made largely inaccessible to Ozzie, of a workforce made up of Microsoft lifers who had become unmotivated millionaires, and of a once-fierce organization now petrified by Google yet unable to mention it as more than "the g-word."

Implied but mostly unsaid in all the blog talk are the roles or nonroles played by founder Bill Gates and current CEO Steve Ballmer in this hoped-for Microsoft reinvention. Ballmer may not be fully on board, observers speculate, and Gates has disembarked. We can't know whether Ozzie's task would have been made easier if Gates and Ballmer escorted change every step of the way, as Intuit's Scott Cook did. But we can guess.

When transformative leaders undertake reinvention, they both lead and follow. That's what happened at Intuit, where founder Cook spurred CEO Bennett to be unstinting in his efforts to introduce Intuit to its future. Cook did this while also continuing to be the keeper of the company flame, which was of great importance to his workforce and aided in achieving their buy-in.

Similarly, Michael Dell deserves credit for his enabling and encouraging role in defeating Dell Hell. Without his full support, the company would not have opened itself to true dialog with its customers—a dialog that has not only aided customer service efforts but has provided the company with a conduit for considering and pretesting product ideas in the marketplace. In that respect, Dell-the-company has gained as much as it has given, and Michael Dell's typically understated approval for the reinvention was crucial in getting there.

Just as the CEO or founder is an underappreciated factor in reinvention, so is time. When crisis isn't the catalyst for change, it would appear that large organizations benefit from two or more years with which to reverse the engines and find a new course. Time allows for the internal discussion necessary to gain the participation of employees. It also allows for prototyping or other sorts of trial efforts, if required.

But none of these reinvention prerequisites—not CEO leadership, nor time, nor employee involvement—is important in the extremely rare companies that have created a culture inherently comfortable with reinvention. One of the best examples of this type is the oldest company mentioned in this book, United Parcel Service (UPS), which has reinvented itself not once or twice, but repeatedly.

STAYING CONSTRUCTIVELY DISSATISFIED

Not all UPS employees wear brown shorts and drive a panel truck anymore. In fact, some of the global shipper's newest employees wear blue, work in some 750 nondescript hangars located in and around airports, and, because their checks say Supply Chain Solutions (SCS), they may not even know they work for UPS. Certainly the end-users they serve don't know the role that UPS plays in their transactions. These consumers think they're dealing with the company that took their online order, or the manufacturer of that electronic device they sent in to be fixed. But the fulfillment and the repairs are being done by UPS, under contract to the shipper or manufacturer.

"Brown" is indisputably the world's largest package delivery company, with revenues as high as $50 billion in 2008. It employs more than 400,000 employees in 200 countries worldwide, but, as you've just seen, UPS does far more than deliver packages these days. UPS now considers its mission "enabling global commerce." So if that means fulfilling orders or hiring technicians capable of fixing electronics, that's what UPS will do, because UPS will accomplish anything in order to enable a corporate customer to improve business and make it faster.

Today's logistics-oriented UPS has come a long way from the bicycle messenger service that began just after the turn of the twentieth century. Today, the vast enterprise bears little resemblance to the shipping company that spent most of its existence fighting the Interstate Commerce Commission for the right to grow. (Believe it or not, it wasn't until 1975 that UPS was able to serve the entire U.S. It took 23 years of state-by-state litigation to get there.)

Decade after decade, UPS has survived waves of change by spotting and staying ahead of each crest. When home telephones came into being and obviated the need for bike messengers, founder Jim Casey shifted the business toward department store deliveries made from his fleet of then-rare cars. When department store deliveries waned, partly because more customers bought cars and became able to drive their own packages home, UPS refashioned itself as the interstate common carrier service we know so well. When FedEx emerged, UPS added international shipping by air and grew to be the world's eighth largest airline. And, when the Internet began to eat away at shipping traffic, UPS began exploring the almost boundless niche known as logistics or supply chain.

At times, the strategic adjustments necessitated by change have been significant. Always a conservative company preferring to play its cards close to the vest, UPS surprised many when it elected to go public in 1991. It did so only to further its reinvention efforts, which required both expansion capital and stock certificates, the latter of which would become the currency for a clutch of planned acquisitions. That's how strongly UPS believes in re-creating itself so it can stand steady in a shifting marketplace—it was even willing to give up its native privacy to do it.

"I think UPS has always been constructively dissatisfied," then-chairman and CEO Michael Eskew told *BusinessWeek* in 2002. "We're always looking for ways to do it better." (Historic note: "Be constructively dissatisfied" was one of founder Casey's favorite workplace aphorisms dating back to 1956.) Eskew, like the CEOs that preceded and followed him, believes that reinvention offers UPS the best way to grow and stay competitive in a highly disruptive marketplace.

UPS's foray into the supply chain market began with small steps before 2000 but became a strategic goal after discussion at a management retreat in 2002. The story was recounted in a 2004 *BusinessWeek* article. Eskew, the champion of the initiative, pointed out that the company's bread-and-butter business, package delivery in the United States, was showing signs of peaking. He produced figures showing that logistics could provide up to 20 percent of UPS's future growth. Competition was assured if the logistics market was breached, but UPS's advantage was decades of experience in managing its own global network—transportation scheduling, storage handling, delivery management, freight forwarding, order fulfillment, and tracking the movement of goods. By performing these tasks for other companies on a contract basis, UPS could help companies "improve their cash flow, their customer service, and their productivity," Eskew said.

Eskew knew that getting there wouldn't be easy, and according to *Business-Week*, he said so in his presentation. To become a player in supply chain, "we will have to change ourselves," he said, matter-of-factly.

Like most UPS executives, Eskew had spent his entire career in the company. He bled brown and knew that what he was suggesting posed certain risks. Logistics is typically a low-margin business—two percent to five percent. But Eskew's bet was that the supply-chain business would bring UPS additional shipping volume for its mainline package-delivery service. That proved true: A year into the effort, UPS was already claiming an additional $2 billion in revenue from shipping realized through logistics clients, and the gains have continued.

Throughout the industry, there are critics who say that UPS will never gain enough new shipping business to compensate for the lower margins of logistics. One of them, not surprisingly, is a rival: FedEx founder and chairman Fred Smith. But UPS is quick to point out that profit margin isn't the only measure of success. Return on investment also tells the story, and logistics is far less capital intensive than package delivery with its costly outlays for trucks, airplanes, real estate, and technology. Still, no one is pretending that reinventing UPS as a supply-chain powerhouse didn't cost money. In the first few years alone, UPS spent more than $1 billion to acquire 25 companies involved in freight forwarding, customs clearance, finance, and other logistics services.

Today's UPS is a shape-shifter, capable of becoming whatever the customer needs it to be:

- For European shoemaker Birkenstock, UPS speeds shipments into stores. Instead of shipping from Germany to California via the Panama Canal, the manufacturer ships to a UPS site on the East Coast. Letting UPS be the drop-shipper cuts transit times from six weeks to three. Birkenstock executives knew they'd permanently ceased handling their own supply chain when, thanks to UPS, merchandise shipped 100 percent on time for the first time ever.
- For Ford Motor Company, UPS maintains a postproduction inventory, puts cars on trains, and, best of all, ensures that they arrive where they're supposed to. Ford used to lose—yes, *lose*—a goodly number of its cars each year to shipping snafus. No more. UPS tracks each car as if it were a box of Omaha Steaks (another UPS logistics customer).
- For fast-paced, high-tech companies, UPS's supply chain services ensure that parts and products don't sit in inventory until they become

irrelevant or obsolete. Using very sophisticated inventory information systems, UPS assists companies such as National Semiconductor in knowing what's in inventory, where it will be going, and when. For another high-tech client, UPS provides critical parts replacement, guaranteeing delivery to businesses within just two to four hours of discovering the problem.

- For smaller companies, UPS offers the chance to maintain a supply chain sophisticated enough to keep pace with the biggest of competitors, at a contract price a small player can afford. AND1, a sports apparel outfit near Philadelphia, gave its entire supply chain to UPS, netting the Nike competitor logistics experts around the globe, the latest inventory tracking technology, and two warehouses in California and Kentucky with which to mount its assault.

- For companies whose business dictates that they offer repairs and service, UPS eliminates two legs of the shipping circuit. Instead of the customer boxing up the equipment and bringing it to UPS, who then sends it to the manufacturer, the merchandise stays with UPS and gets repaired there. It's top-secret stuff much of the time, since manufacturers generally prefer that customers believe that the repairs are done within their own factory walls.

Clearly, UPS is not Jim Casey's package-delivery company anymore. The longtime corporate logo, a shield tied with a ribbon to look like a package, has been replaced with a ribbon-free shield that somehow conveys forward progress without attaching the company to any particular line of business. Advertising slogans have become vague, too. One of the best known tag-lines of the last few years has been "What Can Brown Do for You?" A lot more than it used to be able to do, of course, thanks to its more recent reinventions.

Interestingly enough, UPS has only begun emphasizing the company's tradition of "reinvention"—using that word—in the last 10 years or so. It did so, former CEO Jim Kelly told *Harvard Business Review*, to take away any apprehension that might accompany the prospect of adopting new business strategies. "We began talking about our history in this way to give ourselves a sense of, 'Yeah, it's new and it's different, and it's tough, and it's a change—but that's okay. We've done that successfully for many years.'"

You might wonder, as I did, what UPS does to gain the backing of its employees each time it undertakes one of its reinventions. Is there a specific process it imposes, or is UPS one of those companies that might be tempted to present the reinvention as a crisis that needs to be surmounted, so as to get employees to put a shoulder to the wheel? As its history might suggest, even today, UPS presents its reinventions as opportunities or, at most, challenges.

What's more, that capacity for reinvention starts at the beginning of an employee's career at UPS, with his first day of training.

Training at UPS is detail oriented, right down to telling drivers how to hold their truck keys for maximal efficiency. But the training is also rich in history and tradition "to allow the culture to perpetuate itself," as Kelly has put it. The curriculum also gives trainees a better-than-basic grasp of corporate aims, and that's by design. As Kelly explained it in a 2001 *Harvard Business Review* article, "People need a pretty good understanding of the company's strategy, not just some superficial phrases, if they're going to move together in the right direction." However, perhaps the most impactful segment of training comes near the end, when retired UPS drivers and managers come in to share lore with the new hires and, it is hoped, to instill company pride.

This unusual depth of training is the foundation on which UPS builds all it does, including reinventions. It's also the basis upon which many a UPS career has been built. In fact, all but one of the company's 10 CEOs has been an internal hire. Scott Davis, the current and only exception, nonetheless sees through brown-colored glasses just as his predecessors did.

"It sounds folksy, but we really think the job is to leave the company in better shape for the next generation," Davis told the *Atlanta Constitution-Journal* in 2008, explaining the company's reinvention bias. He points out that UPS has successfully completed a century in business, not by moving the stock price from year to year, but by being "nimble and able to transform." If UPS can continue to do that, Davis says, "We'll be here another hundred years from now, doing the same thing."

Being nimble and able to transform...a company capable of reinvention, one that sheds its skin at will as UPS does, has discovered a competitive advantage too potent to fall into disuse. Such an enterprise takes control of its future and remains transformative for years to come.

Chapter 10

BECOMING *BUILT FOR CHANGE*

How do you make your own company transformative? What steps can you take to improve your chances of becoming *built for change*? It's sometimes difficult to be prescriptive about it, in part because the transformative nature of a company is best seen in hindsight. That's why many of the companies featured in this book are 10 years old or older.

No, becoming transformative is not something you put into a business plan and measure quarterly progress toward. In this final section we'll try to capture a glimpse of what a bound-to-be-transformative company may look like in its formative stages. We won't do it with examples or hypothetical cases, but with questions aimed at helping you and your team find your own answers.

To start, my advice is to pick one chapter, one characteristic of transformation, and focus on it rather than try to tackle all elements at once. You can start with a trait that seems to fit your company, or you can zero in on the one that seems least like your company today but most critical to future success. Just start somewhere that speaks to you. Using the questions I've provided, you can then think about how you might enhance your company's performance in this area.

If you then choose to move on to other characteristics, great, but before you do, try figuring out some additional questions to ask yourselves, or developing some prototypes to test any changes you may be considering. The inquiry process alone is an example of detachment, so I predict you'll see positive results.

QUESTIONS FOR OWNERS AND MANAGERS

Universality: The Common Element

Transformative companies very overtly tap into universal aspirations and needs: hope, knowledge, escape, fun, security, curiosity, significance, empowerment, insight, fame, love, and so forth.

In one word, what fundamental benefit do your customers receive by the very existence of your company?

What aspirations or elemental needs are fulfilled?

How does your internal and external messaging reflect these needs or aspirations?

Does it support or contradict them?

Are these signals overt or hidden?

Are your employees and customers aware of them?

Fearlessness: Risk versus Inevitability

Transformative companies don't perceive risk the way others do. In many cases, they don't even see the same perils as their competitors do. Instead, they rely on acute customer knowledge to provide the unique edge when approaching new opportunities.

Do you use your own product?

How easily could you articulate the value proposition from your customers' perspective?

What customer insights does your company have that no others possess?

Are there things you know about your customers that no one else does?

What opportunities arise from that knowledge?

Process: Templates for Building Creativity and Talent Density

From the outset, transformative companies build for the next generation of employees. They use outlines or templates to encourage creativity and remove controls as complexity increases.

What methods or templates could you instill that would enable someone with half your experience to perform your job twice as effectively?

As your business has grown, has complexity increased your internal controls or has it decreased them?

It's said that company culture is what does the managing when the boss isn't around. How do you instill your company's DNA into your employees so that they can do what is necessary for success with minimal supervision?

Irreverence: Choreographing Your Own Dance

Transformative companies are not distracted by the status quo or industry norms, and they typically measure customer value differently from the way that their competitors do. As a corollary, this work environment creates a self-reinforcing magnetic effect that attracts and retains talented people.

> How is fun measured in your company?
> Are mavericks encouraged or eased out?

Zappos thinks call center efficiency is the wrong metric for a virtual sales company. What accepted industry benchmark do you track that may actually shrink the lifetime value of a customer rather than grow it?

Banishing Small Thinking: Killing the Devil's Advocate

Transformative companies forbid "we don't do it that way" thinking. Multiple levels of employees participate in long-term planning and are expected to think big on behalf of the business.

> Is there an initiative that you've considered but held back on for reasons of tradition?
> Have you ever invoked or tolerated the devil's advocate?
> What is the lowest level in your company where planning extends beyond one year?

Appetite for Destruction: Don't Rock the Boat—Sink It

Transformative companies are absolutely committed to annihilating existing business models and value chains. They are unafraid of empowering customers with greater autonomy and capacity for self-service in order to collapse operating costs.

> If your board fired you tomorrow and you started a new enterprise but could only hire one person from your former company, who would you hire?
> How would you eviscerate your former company's profits?

Caution! Every single transformative company we studied succeeded by giving their customers increased visibility, information, and control over their purchase decisions.

If you are not thinking this way, I promise you your competition is.

Detachment: Proactive Inaction

Transformative companies relax methodically and proactively. They are disciplined about separating from the day-to-day and encourage all levels of employees to gain fresh perspectives on the business.

Do you have a formal process for getting an outsider's view of your business?

Is Think Time formally encouraged and supported?

How is it tracked?

As CEO, do you demonstrate the strategic use of Think Time?

Reinvention: Casting Off Your Own Shadow

Whether in crisis or not, transformative companies habitually reinvent themselves, keeping what's core and moving in new directions. They are always focused on customer needs, rather than their existing capacities.

If you lost your 10 most influential customers tomorrow, how would you get them back or replace them?

When you consider new ventures, do you start with a skills inventory or a customer-needs assessment?

Is there a person or team in your company specifically charged with customer advocacy?

You may not be able to set out a 10-point plan for becoming transformative, but you can try to create the appropriate conditions for your company to grow on its own. You can use the examples within this book to help you grasp not only the goals that lead to transformation but also the environment that nurtures achievement of those goals.

Then, with a liberal amount of bravery, self-belief, and confidence in the people around you, you can base your strategies and tactics not on what's been done before but on what your particular market or set of customers dictates. You can establish ways of stepping back to judge progress, and, through it all, you can work to ensure that you never become so enamored of what your company does that you can't find the will to change some or even all of it. Once you seem to have survived everything that would have killed a lesser company, you will recognize what outsiders have grown to believe about you: You're *built for change*. Yours will have become a transformative company.

BIBLIOGRAPHY

Sources are listed alphabetically by chapter and company.

CHAPTER 2: UNIVERSALITY

Facebook Sources

Barnett, Ruth. "Facebook Group 'Needle in a Haystack' Hopes to Solve Photo Mystery." *Sky News Online,* November 2, 2009. http://news.sky.com/skynews/Home/World-News/Facebook-Group-Needle-In-A-Haystack-Hopes-To-Solve-Photo-Mystery-Camera-Found-In-Mykonos-Greece/Article/200911115429067.

Battelle, John. *The Search: How Google and Its Rivals Rewrote the Rules of Business and Transformed Our Culture.* New York: Penguin, 2005.

Blodget, Henry, "Innovation Series: Mark Zuckerberg." *Business Insider,* February 10, 2010. http://www.businessinsider.com/innovation-series-mark-zuckerberg#ixzz0riKQLziF.

"Brave Thinkers: Mark Zuckerberg of Facebook," *The Atlantic,* November 2009. http://www.theatlantic.com/magazine/archive/2009/11/brave-thinkers/7692/20/.

Ellison, N. B., C. Steinfield, and C. Lampe. "The Benefits of Facebook 'Friends': Social Capital and College Students' Use of Online Social Network Sites." *Journal of Computer-Mediated Communication* 12, no. 4 (2007): article 1. http://jcmc.indiana.edu/vol12/issue4/ellison.html.

Facebook Factbook, August 2009. http://cdn.mashable.com/wp-content/uploads/2010/02/facebook-viz-big.jpg.

Feld, Peter. "Facebook Uses Consumer Feedback To Adapt." *Brandchannel,* October 28, 2009. http://www.brandchannel.com/home/post/2009/10/28/Facebook-Uses-Consumer-Feedback-To-Adapt.aspx#at.

Hoffman, Claire. "The Battle for Facebook." *Rolling Stone,* July 3, 2008. http://web.archive.org/web/20080703220456/http://www.rollingstone.com/news/story/21129674/the_battle_for_facebook/.

Lannin, Sara. "Connections of Strangers Return Camera to Owner," January 22, 2010. http://blog.facebook.com/blog.php?post=252048637130.

Marshall, Matt. "The Evolution of a Remarkable CEO." *Venture Beat,* October 2, 2009. http://venturebeat.com/2009/10/02/mark-zuckerberg-the-evolution-of-a-remarkable-ceo/.

"Oxford Word of the Year 2009: Unfriend." *OUPBlog,* Oxford University Press, November 16, 2009. http://blog.oup.com/2009/11/unfriend/.

Putnam, Robert D. *Bowling Alone: The Collapse and Revival of American Community.* New York: Simon & Shuster, 2000.

Rosenbloom, Stephanie. "On Facebook, Scholars Link Up With Data." *New York Times,* December 17, 2007. http://www.nytimes.com/2007/12/17/style/17facebook.html?_r=1.

Schwartz, Bari. "Hot or Not? Website Briefly Judges Looks." *Harvard Crimson,* November 11, 2004. http://www.thecrimson.com/article.aspx?ref=349808.

Smith, Justin. "Two Years After Facebook Launches News Feed, Sociologists Describe 'Ambient Awareness.'" *Inside Facebook: Tracking Facebook and the Facebook Platform for Developers and Marketers,* September 6, 2008. http://www.insidefacebook.com/2008/09/06/two-years-after-facebook-launches-news-feed-sociologists-describe-ambient-awareness/.

Snider, Mike. "iPods Knock Over Beer Mugs." *USA Today,* June 7, 2006. http://www.usatoday.com/tech/news/2006–06–07-ipod-tops-beer_x.htm.

Tabak, Alan J. "Hundreds Register for New Facebook Website." *Harvard Crimson,* February 9, 2004. http://web.archive.org/web/200504032 15543/www.thecrimson.com/article.aspx?ref=357292.

Thompson, Clive. "I'm So Totally, Digitally Close to You." *New York Times Magazine,* September 7, 2008, p. 42.

LinkedIn.com Sources

Guynn, Jessica. "Professional Networking Site LinkedIn Valued at $1 Billion." *Los Angeles Times,* June 18, 2008. http://www.latimes.com/business/la-fi-linkedin18–2008jun18,0,6631759.story.

"LinkedIn: About Us." http://press.linkedin.com/about.

"LinkedIn: Profile." http://www.thealarmclock.com/mt/archives/2004/08/linkedin_hq_mou.html.

eBay Sources

Ahlee, Hanh, and Malmendier, Ulrike. "Do Consumers Know Their Willingness to Pay? Evidence from eBay Auctions." Stanford University research

paper, October 2, 2005. http://emlab.berkeley.edu/users/webfac/dellavi
gna/e218_f05/malmendier.pdf.

Gunderson, Amy. "The Great Leaders Series: Pierre Omidyar of eBay." *Inc.*,
December 9, 2009. http://www.inc.com/30years/articles/pierre-omidyar.
html.

Hof, Robert D. "Pierre M. Omidyar: The Web for the People." *Business
Week*, December 6, 2004. http://www.businessweek.com/magazine/con
tent/04_49/b3911015_mz072.htm.

Hof, Robert D. "Q&A with eBay's Pierre Omidyar." *Business Week*, December 3, 2001. http://www.businessweek.com/magazine/content/01_49/
b3760605.htm.

"The Power of All of Us." *Inc.*, February 5, 2007. http://www.inc.com/news/
briefs/200702/0205ebay.html.

Taylor, Leslie. "EBay Fuels Growth of Sole Proprietorships," *Inc.*, August 15,
2006. http://www.inc.com/news/articles/200608/self.html.

Starbucks Sources

Bevan, Judi. "CORPORATIONS: Judi Bevan Separates the Froth from the
Caffeine in this Account of a Coffee Superpower." *Sunday Telegraph*
(London), February 17, 2008, p. 55.

Bruzo, Chris. "The Billboard Q&A: Starbucks' Howard Schultz." *Billboard*,
February 16, 2008, p. 27.

Clark, Taylor. *STARBUCKED: A Double Tall Tale of Caffeine, Commerce, and
Culture*. New York: Little, Brown & Company, 2007.

Collins, Clayton. "It's a Starbucks World. (We Only Sip in It.)." *Christian
Science Monitor*, December 18, 2007, p. 15.

Langley, William. "Starbucks: The Choc-Chip Frappuccino That Conquered
the World." *Sunday Telegraph* (London), February 22, 2009. http://www.
telegraph.co.uk/comment/personal-view/4742640/Starbucks-The-choc-
chip-frappuccino-that-conquered-the-world.html.

Maney, Kevin. "How Starbucks Lost Its 'Fidelity.'" *Money*, September 16, 2009.
http://money.cnn.com/2009/09/16/news/companies/kevin_maney_star
bucks.fortune/index.htm.

Munarriz, Rick Aristotle. "This May Be Starbucks' Dumbest Move Ever."
The Motley Fool, September 30, 2009. http://www.fool.com/invest
ing/general/2009/09/30/this-may-be-starbucks-dumbest-move-ever.
aspx.

O'Rourke, P. J. "Venti Capitalists." *The New York Times*, December 16,
2007. http://www.nytimes.com/2007/12/16/books/review/O-Rourke-t.
html?_r=1.

Sweeney, Brody. "How Starbucks Built a Fortune on the Loneliness of Consumers." *The Irish Times,* March 31, 2008. http://www.irishtimes.com/newspaper/innovation/2008/0331/1206752248593.html.

York, Emily Bryson. "How 'Mr. Starbucks' Became Mr. Tether." *Advertising Age,* May 5, 2008, p. 14.

CHAPTER 3: FEARLESSNESS

Blackboard Sources

Burn, Timothy. "Big Man on Campus: Blackboard CEO Michael Chasen Changes the Face of Learning." *Smart CEO,* May 2006. http://library.blackboard.com/docs/Press_Center/CEO_of_the_Year_2006.pdf.

Chasen, Michael. Fox News interview. http://www.foxbusiness.com/search-results/m/22243605/top-grade-for-blackboard.htm#q=Michael+Chasen.

Darcy, Darlene. "A Blackboard Legacy? Years at Blackboard an Education That Turns Employees into Entrepreneurs." *Washington Business Journal,* July 31, 2009, p. 1.

Hart, Kim. "Success of Blackboard and Other Firms Reveals Stability in Local Tech Industry." *Washington Post,* May 14, 2007. http://www.washingtonpost.com/wp-dyn/content/article/2007/05/12/AR2007051201757.html.

Patterson, Andrew. "Blackboard Ruins College." *The Motley Fool,* August 4, 2005. http://www.fool.com/investing/small-cap/2005/08/04/blackboard-ruins-college.aspx.

Pearlstein, Steven. "Here in D.C., the Quiet Rise of a Software Powerhouse." *Washington Post,* May 31, 2006. http://www.washingtonpost.com/wp-dyn/content/article/2006/05/30/AR2006053001259.html.

Wilson, Sara. "Build a Billion-Dollar Business." *Entrepreneur,* March 2009. http://www.entrepreneur.com/magazine/entrepreneur/2009/march/200100.html.

Cirrus Designs Sources

Bertorelli, Paul. "Pre-Production Airplane Deposits: Must Buyers Risk Them?" AviationConsumer.com. http://www.aviationconsumer.com/breakingnews/Pre-Production-Airplane-Deposits.html.

"Dumb Enough to Start and Smart Enough to Finish." *Van Nuys Aviation Journal,* 2007. http://cirrusaircraft.com/about/news/pdf/08.04.VanNuysAviationJournal.pdf.

Fallows, James. "Freedom of the Skies." *The Atlantic,* June 2001. http://www.theatlantic.com/magazine/archive/2001/06/freedom-of-the-skies/2233/.

Fallows, James. "Turn Left at Cloud 109." *New York Times,* November 21, 1999. http://www.nytimes.com/1999/11/21/magazine/turn-left-at-cloud-109.html?pagewanted=all.

"Finding the Right Funding: The Klapmeier Brothers' Key Move," Startup Nation. http://www.startupnation.com/articles/9572/1/Find%20the%20Right%20Business%20Funding.html.

Klapmeier, Alan. Videotaped presentation to Aero Club of Atlanta, January 2009. http://video.realviewtv.com/aviation/aeroclub_alan_klapmeier_cirrus/.

Charles Schwab Sources

"The Charles Schwab Corporation." *Funding Universe.* http://www.funding universe.com/company-histories/The-Charles-Schwab-Corporation-Company-History.html.

De Bono, Edward, and Rolbert Heller. "Revolutionary Strategies: Forget about Evolving at Your Own Pace and Develop Revolutionary Strategies." *Thinking Managers,* July 8, 2006. http://www.thinkingmanagers.com/management/revolutionary-strategies.php.

"History." Charles Schwab Web site. http://www.aboutschwab.com/about/history/index.html.

Kador, John. *Charles Schwab: How One Company Beat Wall Street and Reinvented the Brokerage Industry.* Hoboken, NJ: John Wiley and Sons, 2002.

Lyons, Nancy. "The Disruptive Start-Up: Clayton Christensen on How to Compete with the Best." *Inc.,* February 1, 2002. http://www.inc.com/magazine/20020201/23854_pagen_1.html.

Slywotzy, Adrian J., and David J. Morrison. *The Profit Zone: How Strategic Business Design Will Lead You to Tomorrow's Profits.* New York: Random House, 2002.

Amazon Sources

Burrows, Peter. "Bezos on Innovation." *Business Week,* April 17, 2008. http://www.businessweek.com/magazine/content/08_17/b4081064880218.htm.

Davidson, Andrew. "Amazon Chief Shoots For Stars." *Sunday Times* (London), November 11, 2007, p. 6.

"Jeff Bezos Interview." *The Charlie Rose Show,* February 26, 2009. http://www.charlierose.com/view/interview/10105.

Levy, Steven. "Jeff Bezos." *Newsweek,* January 5, 2009. http://www.newsweek.com/id/70983/page/1.

Milliot, Jim. "PW's Person of the Year: Amazon's Jeff Bezos, Love Him or Hate Him, He Has Made a Difference." *Publishers Weekly,* December 8, 2008, p. 24.

Quittner, Josh. "The Charmed Dot-Com Life of Jeff Bezos." *Fortune,* April 2008. http://money.cnn.com/2008/04/14/news/companies/quittner_bezos.fortune/index.htm.

Quittner, Josh. "How Jeff Bezos Rules the Retail Space." *Fortune,* May 5, 2008, p. 126.

Solomon, Debra. "Book Learning: Questions for Jeffrey P. Bezos." *New York Times,* December 2, 2009. http://www.nytimes.com/2009/12/06/magazine/06fob-q4-t.html.

Stone, Brad. "Sold On eBay, Shipped by Amazon.com." *New York Times,* April 27, 2007. http://www.nytimes.com/2007/04/27/technology/27amazon.html.

CHAPTER 4: PROCESS

Boston Brewing Company (BBC) Sources

BBC. "Best Job in the World" commercial. http://www.youtube.com/watch?v=w9NTHuQbJXo.

BBC. "Noble Hops" commercial. http://www.youtube.com/watch?v=3U8GatI37kQ.

"The Boston Beer Company: About Us." http://www.bostonbeer.com/phoenix.zhtml?c=69432&p=irol-homeProfile.

Fenton, Matthew, and David Wecker. "Sam Adams: A Beer with a Filling Story." *Business Courier* (Cincinnati, Ohio), September 7, 2007. http://cincinnati.bizjournals.com/cincinnati/stories/2007/09/10/smallb2.html.

Fimrite, Peter. "Joseph Owades: Brewmaster, Created Light Beer." *San Francisco Chronicle,* December 20, 2005. http://articles.sfgate.com/2005-12-20/bay-area/17405023_1_joseph-l-owades-samuel-adams-boston-lager-beer.

Mamis, Robert A. "Market Maker." *Inc.,* December 1, 1995. http://www.inc.com/magazine/19951201/2510.html.

Chipotle Grill Sources

Brand, Rachel. "Chipotle Founder Had Big Dreams." *Rocky Mountain News,* December 23, 2006. http://www.rockymountainnews.com/drmn/other_business/article/0,2777,DRMN_23916_5233690,00.html.

Chipotle Mexican Grill, Inc. *Funding Universe.* http://www.fundinguniverse.com/company-histories/Chipotle-Mexican-Grill-Inc-Company-History.html.

Cohen, Arianne. "Ode to a Burrito." *Fast Company*, April 1, 2008. http://www.fastcompany.com/magazine/124/ode-to-a-burrito.html?page=0%2C1.

"McDonald's Plans to Reduce Ownership of Chipotle Grill." *Design and Display Ideas*, April 27, 2006. http://www.allbusiness.com/retail-trade/miscellaneous-retail/4440581-1.html.

Zappos Sources

McDonald, Duff. "Open Source's Sole Purpose." *CIO Insight*, November 10, 2006. http://www.cioinsight.com/c/a/Case-Studies/Case-Study-Fast-Simple-OpenSource-IT/.

Weisul, Kimberly. "A Shine on Their Shoes." *Business Week*, December 5, 2005, p. 84.

Cognizant Sources

Cognizant Two-in-a-Box. http://www.cognizant.com/html/approach/Two_in_a_Box.pdf.

Cognizant 2.0. http://www.cognizant.com/html/approach/cognizant-2.0.asp.

Jayashankar, Mitu, and N. S. Ramnath. "Cognizant: Fixing it Before it's Broke." *Forbes India*, January 25, 2010. http://business.in.com/article/board room/fixing-it-before-its-broke/9472/1.

Netflix Sources

Heath, Chip, and Dan Heath. *Made to Stick: Why Some Ideas Survive and Others Die*. New York: Random House, 2008.

"Management." Netflix. http://ir.netflix.com/management.cfm.

Netflix Human Resources Slide Set. http://www.techcrunch.com/2009/08/05/other-companies-should-have-to-read-this-internal-netflix-presentation/.

"Netflix's Autonomous Workforce." *Fast Company*, March 27, 2007. http://www.fastcompany.com/blog/fast-company-staff/fast-company-blog/netflixs-autonomous-workforce.

Schneider, Laura. "Netflix: Company Profile." http://jobsearchtech.about.com/od/companyprofiles/a/Netflix.htm.

CHAPTER 5: IRREVERENCE

Southwest Airlines Sources

Bailey, Jeff. "Southwest. Way Southwest." *New York Times*, February 2008. http://www.nytimes.com/2008/02/13/business/13southwest.html?_r=1&ref=gary_c_kelly.

Pavese, Antonella. "No Fear of Flying Southwest." Author's blog, June 11, 2006. http://www.antonellapavese.com/2006/06/11/no-fear-of-flying-southwest/#more-187.

Richter, Millie. "An Optimized Halloween." *Nuts About Southwest.* Blog, October 29, 2009. http://www.blogsouthwest.com/blog/an-optimized-halloween.

Southwest. Youtube Video of Toilet Roll Races. http://www.youtube.com/watch?v=ZjikovLphCI.

Southwest. Youtube Video of "We Give You Peanuts." http://www.youtube.com/watch?v=DDpPPw4QMqM&feature=related.

Taylor, Fred. "How Southwest's Culture Drives Cost Leadership." Speech given for OPG Business Leadership Program, Amsterdam, The Netherlands, December 8, 2008. http://www.southwest.com/swamedia/speeches/fred_taylor_speech.pdf.

Zappos Sources

Chafkin, Max. "The Zappos Way of Managing." *Inc.,* May 2009. http://www.inc.com/magazine/20090501/the-zappos-way-of-managing.html/.

Djambazov, Angel. "Endless Two-Step: Real reason Amazon bought Zappos." *ReveNews,* July 23, 2009. http://www.revenews.com/angeldjambazov/endless-two-step-real-reason-amazon-bought-zappos/.

Durst, Sidra. "Shoe In." *Business 2.0,* December 2006, p. 54.

Gentry, Connie. "Cultural Revolution." *Chain Store Age,* December 2007. http://www.chainstoreage.com/industrydata/pdfs/rsoy/CSA_2007_EOY.pdf.

Gergen, Christopher, and Gregg Vanourek. "Zappos Culture Sows Spirit." *Washington Times,* July 16, 2008. http://www.washingtontimes.com/news/2008/jul/16/zappos-culture-sows-spirit/.

Gordhamer, Soren. "The New Social Engagement: A Visit to Zappos." *Mashable/Business,* April 26, 2009. http://mashable.com/2009/04/26/zappos/.

McFarland, Keith. "Why Zappos Offers New Hires $2,000 a Week to Quit." *Business Week,* September 17, 2008.

O'Brien, Jeffrey M. "Zappos Knows How to Kick It." *Fortune,* February 2, 2009, p. 54.

"Other Employee-Customer Fun." Zappos Box-Day videos. http://about.zappos.com/.

"Thank-You Note from Janet E." Zappos. http://www.zappos.com/testimonial/page/1/start/20.

Wilson, Sara. "Build a Billion Dollar Business." *Entrepreneur,* March 2009, p. 44.

Zaczkiewicz, Arthur. "Zappos Sells Service." *WWD,* November 15, 2006. http://www.wwd.com/fashion-news/zappos-sells-service-516777.

Zmuda, Natalie. "Zappos: Customer Service First and a Daily Obsession." *Advertising Age,* October 20, 2008, p. 36.

Springfield Manufacturing (SRC) Sources

Amend, Patricia. "The Turnaround." *Inc.*, August 1986. http://www.inc.com/magazine/19860801/15640_pagen_1.html.

Burlingham, Bo. "America's 25 Most Fascinating Entrepreneurs: Jack Stack, SRC." *Inc.,* April 2004. http://www.inc.com/magazine/20040401/25stack.html.

Case, John. "The Open-Book Revolution." *Inc.,* June 1, 1995. http://www.inc.com/magazine/19950601/2296.html.

Stack, Jack. *The Great Game of Business.* New York: Doubleday, 1994.

Google Sources

"Life at Google." Google Web site. http://www.google.com/jobs/lifeatgoogle/.

"Working at Google: Brainstorming @ Google." Embedded video in "How to Organize a Brainstorming Session." *Happy Brainstorming.* http://happybrainstorm.com/index.php/How-to-organise-a-BRAINSTORMING-session.html.

AstraZeneca and Genentech Source

Kling, Jim. "The University in Corporate Clothing." *Science* (Science Careers), September 9, 2005. http://sciencecareers.sciencemag.org/career_magazine/previous_issues/articles/2005_09_09/noDOI.17890754345905885212.

Wieden + Kennedy Source

Berger, Warren. "America's 25 Most Fascinating Entrepreneurs: Dan Wieden." *Inc.,* April 2004. http://www.inc.com/magazine/20040401/25wieden.html.

CHAPTER 6: BANISHING SMALL THINKING
Amazon Sources

Amazon 1997 Letter to Shareholders. http://www.corporate-ir.net/ireye/ir_site.zhtml?ticker=AMZN&script=10903&layout=8&item_id=%27

http://media.corporate-ir.net/media_files/NSD/AMZN/reports/97ar_letter.htm%27.

Burrows, Peter. "Bezos: How Frugality Drives Innovation." *Business Week,* April 28, 2008, p. 64.

Hof, Robert D. "Jeff Bezos' Risky Bet." *Business Week,* November 13, 2006, p. 52.

"Jeff Bezos Interview." *The Charlie Rose Show,* February 26, 2009. http://www.charlierose.com/view/interview/10105.

Johnson, Christopher. "Amazon: The River, Not the Woman Warrior." *The Name Inspector,* February 19, 2007. http://www.thenameinspector.com/amazon/.

Quittner, Josh. "How Jeff Bezos Rules the Retail Space." *Fortune,* May 5, 2008, p. 126.

Stone, Brad. "Sold on eBay, Shipped by Amazon." *New York Times,* April 27, 2007. http://www.nytimes.com/2007/04/27/technology/27amazon.html.

Vogelstein, Fred. "Mighty Amazon." *Fortune,* May 26, 2003, p. 60.

Netflix Sources

Boyle, Matthew. "Questions for Reed Hastings." *Money,* May 28, 2007, p. 30.

McMillan, Doug. "Netflix, AT&T Are Real Winners of Netflix Prize." *Business Week,* September 21, 2009. http://www.businessweek.com/the_thread/techbeat/archives/2009/09/netflix_att_are.html.

Netflix Prize Competition Web page. http://www.netflixprize.com//community/viewtopic.php?id=1520.

Think Big Kansas City. "A Million Reasons to Think Big." Contains embedded video interview with Reed Hastings, Netflix founder/CEO, January 19, 2010. http://thinkbigkansascity.com/component/wordpress/?author=62.

Intuit Source

Taylor, Suzanne, and Kathy Schroeder. *Inside Intuit.* Cambridge, MA: Harvard Business School Publishing, 2003.

Google Source

Battelle, John. *The Search: How Google and Its Rivals Rewrote the Rules of Business and Transformed Our Culture.* New York: Penguin, 2005.

Jarvis, Jeff. *What Would Google Do?* New York: Harper-Collins, 2009.

Kelley, Tom, and Jonathan Littman. *Ten Faces of Innovation: IDEO's Strategies for Defeating the Devil's Advocate and Driving Creativity Throughout Your Organization.* New York: Doubleday, 2005.

Morrison, Chris. "How to Innovate Like Apple." BNET (CBS Interactive), August 10, 2009. http://www.bnet.com/2403–13501_23–330240.html.

CHAPTER 7: APPETITE FOR DESTRUCTION

Craigslist Sources

Coll, Steve. "Think Tank: Nonprofit Newspapers." *The New Yorker,* January 28, 2009. http://www.newyorker.com/online/blogs/stevecoll/2009/01/non profit-newsp.html.

Harris, Paul. "America's Most Revered Newspaper is Latest to be Hit with Financial Woes." *The Observer,* January 11, 2009. http://www.guardian.co.uk/media/2009/jan/11/new-york-times-credit-crunch.

Kamer, Foster. "Pretty Graph Chart Shows Print Journalism's Ugly Downfall." *Gawker,* September 6, 2009. http://gawker.com/5368584/pretty-graph-chart-shows-print-journalisms-ugly-downfallhttp://www.mint.com/blog/trends/the-death-of-the-newspaper/.

Swarts, Will. "Craigslist: Stopping the Presses?" *Smart Money* (*Wall Street Journal* digital edition), September 7, 2005. http://www.smartmoney.com/investing/stocks/craigslist-stopping-the-presses-18189/.

Weiss, Philip. "A Guy Named Craig." *New York,* January 16, 2006, p. 26.

American Idol Sources

Baker, Bob. "What's Wrong with American Idol?" *The Buzz Factor.* http://bob-baker.com/buzz/american-idol-wrong.html.

Bauder, David. "'Idol' Attracts More Than 32M Viewers." *The Washington Post,* January 30, 2007. http://www.washingtonpost.com/wp-dyn/content/article/2007/01/30/AR2007013001098.html?nav=rss_artsandliving/entertainmentnews.

Carter, Bill. "For Fox's Rivals, 'American Idol' Remains a 'Schoolyard Bully.'" *New York Times,* February 20, 2007. http://www.nytimes.com/2007/02/20/arts/television/20idol.html?_r=1.

Markunas, Jim. "Is A&R Still Necessary in Today's Music Industry?" *Music Think Tank,* May 2, 2009. http://www.musicthinktank.com/blog/is-ar-still-necessary-in-todays-music-industry.html.

Marsden, Dr. Paul. "American Idol as Your Business Model." Slide set. http://www.slideshare.net/paulsmarsden/american-idol-as-your-business-model.

Sandall, Robert. "Bank Your Lucky Stars." *Sunday Times* (London), December 8, 2002. http://www.timesonline.co.uk/tol/life_and_style/article836672.ece.

Smith, Caspar Llewellyn. "The Idol Maker." *Blender's The Guide,* February 15, 2004. http://www.blender.com/guide/67382/idol-maker.html.

Wansell, Geoffrey. "This Man Wants to Rule the World." *Evening Standard,* April 18, 2002. http://www.thisislondon.co.uk/music/article894171-details/This+man+wants+to+rule+the+world/article.do.

Weisman, Loren. "American Idol Take 2 or Another Take." *Music Think Tank,* August 5, 2009. http://www.musicthinktank.com/mtt-open/2009/8/5/american-idol-take-2-or-another-take.html.

Apple Sources

Borland, John. "Music Moguls Trumped by Steve Jobs?" *CNET.com,* April 15, 2005. http://news.cnet.com/Music-moguls-trumped-by-Steve-Jobs/2100–1027_3–5671705.html.

Johnson, Mark W., Clayton Christensen, and Henning Kagermann. "Reinventing Your Business Model." *Harvard Business Review,* December 2008. http://viewswire.eiu.com/index.asp?layout=EBArti.

Paczkowski, John. "'Apple Has Destroyed the Music Business'—Not That We Didn't Try Our Best." *Digital Daily,* October 9, 2007. http://digitaldaily.allthingsd.com/20071029/apple-destroyed-music-business/cleVW3&article_id=2014007586&rf=0.

Pfanner, Eric. "Music Sales Worldwide Fall by 7 Percent." *New York Times,* January 15, 2009. http://www.nytimes.com/2009/01/15/technology/15iht-digital.4–408839.html.

Sooman, Derek. "Steve Jobs Attacks Record Firms." *Techspot.com,* September 21, 2005. http://www.techspot.com/news/18808-steve-jobs-attacks-record-firms.html.

Amazon Sources

Amazon 2007 Letter to Shareholders. http://g-ecx.images-amazon.com/images/G/01/digital/fiona/general/2007letter.pdf.

Burrows, Peter. "Bezos: How Frugality Drives Innovation." *Business Week,* April 28, 2008, p. 64.

"Jeff Bezos Interview." *The Charlie Rose Show,* February 26, 2009. http://www.charlierose.com/view/interview/10105.

Quittner, Josh. "The 2008 Time 100." *Time,* April 30, 2009. http://www.time.com/time/specials/2007/article/0,28804,1733748_1733758_1736345,00.html.

"Unbound: Book Publishing in America." *The Economist,* June 5, 2008.

CHAPTER 8: DETACHMENT

Microsoft Sources

Gates, Bill. "The Internet Tidal Wave." Exhibit in *U.S. v. Microsoft,* May 26, 1995. http://www.justice.gov/atr/cases/exhibits/20.pdf.

Taylor, Suzanne, and Kathy Schroeder. *Inside Intuit.* Cambridge, MA: Harvard Business School Publishing, 2003.

Amazon Sources

Bjerklie, Steve. "What Are They Worth?" *MetroActive Arts.* (Contains Bill Graham quotation.) http://www.metroactive.com/papers/sfmetro/03.97/rock-art-97–3.html.

Bossidy, Larry, and Ram Charan. *Execution: The Discipline of Getting Things Done.* New York: Crown Business, 2002.

Hightower, Raymond. "Everything I Know by Jeff Bezos." *The Wisdom Blog.* The Wisdom Group, July 23, 2009. http://www.wisdomgroup.com/blog/everything_i_know_by_jeff_bezos/.

"Jeff Bezos Interview." *The Charlie Rose Show,* February 26, 2009. http://www.charlierose.com/view/interview/10105.

Netflix Sources

Netflix management. http://ir.netflix.com/management.cfm.

Vara, Renn. "Moving the Needle at Netflix: Interview with Steve Swasey." *More Than Talk: Conversations about Executive Communications.* SNP Communications, June 8, 2007. http://www.snpnet.com/morethantalk/2007/06/08/moving-the-needle-at-netflix/.

AstraZeneca and Genentech Sources

Astra Zeneca career opportunities Web page. http://careers.astrazeneca.co.uk/.

Genentech Corporate Culture, video. http://ecorner.stanford.edu/authorMaterialInfo.html?mid=1578.

Genentech Scientist Statements. http://www.gene.com/gene/research/sci-profiles/neurosci/t-lavigne/profile.html http://www.gene.com/gene/research/sci-profiles/neurosci/sheng/.

"Genentech's Work Culture and Practices." Case study, IBS Center for Management Research, 2006. http://www.icmrindia.org/casestudies/catalogue/Human%20Resource%20and%20Organization%20Behavior/HROB091.htm.

Hanshaw, Susan. "Why Is Genentech # 2 On CNNMoney.com's 100 Best Companies To Work For In 2007 List?" *InnerArchitect,* January 24, 2008.

http://innerarchitect.wordpress.com/2008/01/24/why-is-genentech-2-on-cnnmoneycoms-100-best-companies-to-work-for-in-2007-list/.

Kling, Jim. "The University in Corporate Clothing." *Science* (Science Careers), September 9, 2005. http://sciencecareers.sciencemag.org/career_magazine/previous_issues/articles/2005_09_09/noDOI.17890754345905885212.

Morris, Betsy. "*Fortune*'s 100 Best Companies to Work For: Genentech is Best Place to Work Now." January 20, 2006. http://money.cnn.com/2006/01/06/news/companies/bestcos_genentech/index.htm.

Google Sources (20 Percent Time)

Atlassian's FedEx Days. http://blogs.atlassian.com/developer/fedex/.

Berkun, Scott. "Thoughts on Google's 20 Percent Time." Author's blog, March 12, 2008. http://www.scottberkun.com/blog/2008/thoughts-on-googles-20-time/.

Facebook Hackathons. http://www.businessinsider.com/mark-zuckerberg-innovation-2009–10.

Other Sources

Allen, Colin. "The Benefits of Meditation." *Psychology Today,* April 2003. http://www.psychologytoday.com/articles/200304/the-benefits-meditation.

Broughton, Philip Delves. "Zen and Success at Work." *London Evening Standard,* May 10, 2009. http://www.thisislondon.co.uk/lifestyle/article-23752437-zen-and-success-at-work.do.

Der Hovanesian, Mara. "Zen and the Art of Corporate Productivity." *Business Week,* July 28, 2003. http://www.businessweek.com/magazine/content/03_30/b3843076.htm.

Ferrazzi, Keith. *Never Eat Alone.* New York: Broadway Business, 2005.

Garlinghouse, Brad. "Yahoo Memo: The 'Peanut Butter Manifesto.'" *Wall Street Journal,* November 18, 2006. http://online.wsj.com/public/article/SB116379821933826657–0mbjXoHnQwDMFH_PVeb_jqe3Chk_20061125.html.

Harnish, Verne. *Mastering the Rockefeller Habits.* New York: SelectBooks, 2002.

Manallack, Stephen. "Meditation Makes You a Better Business Leader." *Domain-B,* August 29, 2009. http://www.domain-b.com/management/general/20090829_stephen_manallack_oneView.html.

Sagmeister, Steven. "The Power of Time Off." *TED Talk,* July 2009. http://www.ted.com/talks/stefan_sagmeister_the_power_of_time_off.html.

CHAPTER 9: REINVENTION

Dell Sources

Cassingham, Randy. "Dell Hell." *This is True* blog. http://www.thisistrue.com/dellhell.html.

Fung, Mei Lin. "You Can Learn From 'Dell Hell.' Dell Did." Institute of Service Organization Excellence, Inc., March 11, 2008. http://www.customerthink.com/user/mei_lin_fung.

Hind, Dominique. "Dell Ideastorm: Community Involvement." Slide set, September 2008. http://www.slideshare.net/DomHind/dell-ideastorm-community-involvement-presentation.

"Hot Laptop" (video). http://www.engadget.com/2006/06/22/dude-your-dell-is-on-fire/.

Jarvis, Jeff. "Dell Learns to Listen." *Business Week,* October 17, 2007, p. 118.

Lithium-Ion Battery Recall. http://en.wikipedia.org/wiki/Lithium-ion_battery.

Livingston, Geoff. "Dell's Incredible Turnaround." *Now Is Gone* blog, October 18, 2007. http://nowisgone.com/2007/10/18/dells-incredible-turnaround/.

Menchaca, Lionel. "Direct2Dell One Year Later." *Direct2Dell* blog, July 14, 2007. http://en.community.dell.com/blogs/direct2dell/archive/2007/07/14/20884.aspx.

Hilti Sources

Johnson, Mark W., Clayton Christensen, and Henning Kagermann. "Reinventing Your Business Model." *Harvard Business Review,* December 2008. http://viewswire.eiu.com/index.asp?layout=EBArticleVW3&article_id=2014007586&rf=0.

Palmer, Sara. "Hilti Strives to Save Companies Money." *Building Design News*(UK). http://www.buildingdesign-news.co.uk/2009/21-Hilti-Anchors-Chemical-anchors-Firestopping-Drilling-260509.asp.

Intuit Sources

Intuit, video interview with CEO Scott Cook. http://ippblog.intuit.com/blog/sandcloud/.

Taylor, Suzanne, and Kathy Schroeder. *Inside Intuit.* Cambridge, MA: Harvard Business School Publishing, 2003.

Microsoft Sources

Gralla, Preston. "Why Has Ray Ozzie Failed at Microsoft?" *Computerworld* blog, October 12, 2009. http://blogs.computerworld.com/14897/why_ has_ray_ozzie_failed_at_microsoft.

Gralla, Preston. "Is Ray Ozzie on the Way Out at Microsoft?" *Computerworld* blog, December 14, 2009. http://blogs.computerworld.com/15253/is_ ray_ozzie_on_the_way_out_at_microsoft.

Levy, Steven. "Ray Ozzie Wants to Push Microsoft Back Into Startup Mode." *Wired,* November 24, 2008. http://www.wired.com/techbiz/people/ magazine/16–12/ff_ozzie?currentPage=2#ixzz0iY09jI4Y.

Patrizio, Andy. "Microsoft's Ray Ozzie on the Hot Seat." *Internet News,* June 16, 2006. http://www.internetnews.com/ent-news/article.php/3613856.

UPS Sources

Benjamin, Matthew. "Out of the Box." *U.S. News & World Report,* January 26, 2004, electronic edition, p. 2.

Foust, Dean. "Big Brown's New Bag." *Business Week,* July 19, 2004, p. 54.

Hira, Nadira A. "The Making of a UPS Driver." *Fortune,* November 12, 2007, p. 118.

Kirby, Julia. "Reinvention with Respect: An Interview with Jim Kelly of UPS." *Harvard Business Review,* November 2001, p. 32.

Lukas, Paul, and Maggie Overfelt. "UPS." *Fortune Small Business,* April 2003. http://money.cnn.com/magazines/fsb/fsb_archive/2003/04/01/341024/ index.htm.

"Q&A: The Man Who's Repackaging UPS." *Business Week,* June 3, 2002, p. 30B.

Ramos, Rachel Tobin. "Q&A: Scott Davis, Chief Executive officer of UPS." *Atlanta Journal-Constitution,* September 20, 2008, p. C1.

Salter, Chuck. "Surprise Package." *Fast Company,* February 2004, p. 62.

INDEX

Amazon: appetite for destruction of, 7, 81–83; banishing small thinking by, 7, 64–67, 74; Kindle reader development, 31–32, 81–82, 85; name derivation, 64–65; obsession with customers, 31–33; purchase of Zappos, 57. *See also* Bezos, Jeff

American Idol: appetite for destruction of, 7, 77–80; hatred of, 77–78; as pop music driving force, 80; pop stardom dream creation by, 77; vs. newspapers, 75. *See also* Cowell, Simon; Fuller, Simon

Andressen, Marc, 87

Antiques Road Show tv show, 17

Appetite for destruction, 75–84; of Amazon, 7, 81–83; of *American Idol,* 7, 77–80; of Apple, 7; of Craigslist/Craig Newmark, 7, 76–77; and customers, 75, 82–84; described, 7; and empowerment strategies, 109; Jeff Jarvis's thoughts about, 76; questions for owners and managers, 109; representation by Shiva, 75; of Steve Jobs, 80–81

Apple: appetite for destruction of, 7, 80–81; meditation for employees at, 92; vs. the music industry, 75. *See also* Jobs, Steve

AstraZeneca, meditation for employees at, 92

Ballmer, Steve, 100

Banishing small thinking, 63–74; by Amazon, 7, 64–67, 74; by Cisco Systems, 73–74; and company-wide long-term thinking, 74; and customers, 7, 66–67, 69–70, 73; by David Humber, Ciena Corp., 63–64; described, 6–7; by Facebook, 7; by Google, 6–7, 71–73; by Intuit software company, 7, 68–71; by Netflix, 7, 67–68; questions for owners and managers, 109; representation by Shiva, 63

Bennett, Steve, 99–100

Bezos, Jeff: appetite for destruction of, 7, 81–83; banishing small thinking by, 7, 64–67, 74; fearlessness displayed by, 31–33; interview with Charlie Rose, 81–82; Kindle reader development, 31–32, 81–82, 85; long-term thinking of, 66; naming of Amazon, 64–65; periodic disappearances of, 85; purchase of Zappos, 57

Blackboard software company: detached reflection by, 88; development of, 23–26, 31, 89; educational adoption of, 24–25; fearlessness of, 4, 23–26, 29; obsession with customers, 31–33. *See also* Chasen, Michael; Pittinsky, Matthew

Bossidy, Larry, 86

Boston Beer Company: Koch's process decisions for, 5, 35–39; letting go, for gaining control by, 41

Bowling Alone (Putnam), 13

Branding: by Amazon, 66; Google's avoidance of, 71; by Radio Shack, 98; by Sam Adams beer, 35–36; self-diluting by Starbucks, 21; by Simon Fuller *(American Idol),* 78–80; by Southwest Airlines, 52; universality of eBay, 18; by Zappos shoes, 52

Brin, Sergey, 11

Burger King fast food chain, 39

Cameron, Danny, 14–15

Casey, Jim, 102, 104. *See also* United Parcel Service (UPS)

Chasen, Michael, 23–26, 29, 31–33, 88. *See also* Blackboard software company

Chipotle Grill: Ells's process decisions for, 5, 39–40; limit-setting by, 39–40; nonprocess processes of, 45. *See also* Ells, Steve

Chrysalis Records, 79

Ciena Corp., 63–64

Cirrus Aviation: can't lose market estimation of, 4; development of, 26–29, 31. *See also* Klapmeier, Alan

Cisco Systems, 73–74

Clarkson, Kelly, 78

Cognizant Technology Solutions: Cognizant University, 41–42; communication platform of, 43–44; detached reflection by, 8, 89–91; process decisions made by, 5, 41–44; two-in-a-box client model, 42–43. *See also* D'Souza, Francisco

Cognizant University, 41–42

Coldplay, 78

Cook, Scott, 98–100. *See also* Intuit software company

Cowell, Simon, 78

Craigslist: appetite for destruction of, 7, 76–77; vs. newspapers, 75, 76. *See also* Newmark, Craig

Customer identification, 31–33

Customers: appetite for destruction and, 75, 82–84; banishing small thinking and, 7, 66–67, 69–70, 73; detachment and, 8, 87–91; fearlessness and, 4, 24, 26, 28–31; irreverence and, 6, 51–57, 59–61; obsession with, 31–33; process and, 5, 37–44, 46; questions for owners/managers about, 108–10; reinvention and, 8, 95–104; and "third place" concept, 19–20; universality and, 12

Davis, Scott, 105. *See also* United Parcel Service

Daydreaming, 93–94

Dell, Michael and Dell Computers, 8, 95–97, 100–101

Detachment (and reflection), 85–94; of Amazon, 7–8; of Bill Gates, Microsoft, 7–8, 85–88; and customers, 8, 87–91; described, 7–8; of D'Souza, Cognizant Technologies, 8, 89–91; of Facebook, 92; of Google, 91–92; of Michael Chasen, Blackboard, 88; of Netflix, 88–89; for problem solving, 87–89; questions for owners and managers, 109–10; reasons for, 86–87; representation by Shiva, 85

Digital connections, on a global scale, 13–15

Direct2Dell.com Web site, 95–96

D'Souza, Francisco, 41–44, 46; detached reflection by, 8, 89–91. *See also* Cognizant Technology Solutions

Dunn, Eric, 69–71. *See also* Intuit software company

eBay, universality of, 12, 17–19

Ells, Steve, 5, 39–40. *See also* Chipotle Grill

Empowerment strategies: and appetite for destruction, 109; by Charles Schwab, 30–31; by Cognizant, 42, 44, 45–46; for the free agency economy, 15–17; by Jack Stack (SRC), 57, 59; by LinkedIn, 4, 11, 16–17, 30; by Netflix, 44, 45–46; universality and, 107

Entrepreneurial vision: of Alan Klapmeier, 26–29, 31; of Charles Schwab, 29–31; of Chasen and Pittinsky, 23–26, 31; of Craig Newmark, 7, 76–77; of Henry Ford, 33; of Jeff Bezos, 31–33, 81–83, 87; of Jim Koch, 5, 35–39, 41; of Reed Hastings, 67–68; of Simon Fuller, 78–80, 84

Eskew, Michael, 102–3

"Everything I Know" speech (Bezos), 85

Excite, 11

Execution, the Discipline of Getting Things Done (Bossidy), 86

Facebook: banishing small thinking by, 7; "connection" represented by, 13; detached reflection by, 92; distinctions from LinkedIn, 16; origin of, 14; universality of, 4

Fearlessness, 23–33; of Blackboard, 4, 23–26, 31, 89; of Charles Schwab, 29–31; of Cirrus Aviation, 4, 26–29, 31; customer identification characteristic, 31–33; and customers, 4, 24, 26, 28–31; described, 4–5; questions for owners and managers, 108; representation by Shiva, 23

FedEx, reinvention by, 97

Ferrazzi, Keith, 93

Ford, Henry, 33

Fox TV network, 80

Fuller, Simon, 78–80, 84

Garlinghouse, Brad, 94

Gates, Bill: "The Internet Tidal Wave" strategy, 85; proactive inaction strategy, 86; reinvention at Microsoft by, 100; Think Week policy, 7, 85, 87

Google: accomplishments of, 71–73; banishing small thinking by, 6–7, 71–73; brainstorming of ideas at, 60; detached reflection by, 91–92; meditation for employees at, 92; origins of, 11; as synonym for Internet searching, 13; universality of, 4. *See also* Brin, Sergey; Page, Larry; *What Would Google Do?*

Graham, Bill, 86–87

Grainge, Lucien, 79

Grateful Dead, 86–87

Hainsworth, Stanley, 19–20, 19–21

Hardcastle, Paul, 79

Harnish, Verne, 94

Hastings, Reed, 44–45, 67–68. *See also* Netflix (DVD company)

Heath, Chip, 47

Heath, Dan, 47

Hilti Fleet Management, 8, 97–98

Hindu ideas. *See* meditation for employees; Shiva symbolism

Holy Grail of business, 12

Hsieh, David, 73–74. *See also* Cisco Systems

Hsieh, Tony, 53–57. *See also* Zappos (online shoe retailer)

Huber, David, 63–64, 74

Inside Intuit (Taylor & Schroeder), 98–99

"The Internet Tidal Wave" strategy (of Bill Gates), 85

Intuit software company, 68–71, 98–100. *See also* Bennett, Steve; Cook, Scott

iPad (Apple), 81

Irreverence, 49–62; and committed employees, 59–60; and customers, 6, 51–57, 59–61; described, 5–6;

and individuality/autonomy, 61; and internal decision making, 60–61; questions for owners and managers, 108–9; representation by Shiva, 49; by Southwest Airlines, 5–6, 49–52; by Springfield Remanufacturing Corp., 6, 57–59; by SRC, 6; and toleration for mistakes, 61; by Zappos, 5, 6, 52–57, 62
iTunes vs. CD sales, 80–81

Jarvis, Jeff, 73, 76, 95
Jobs, Steve, 80–81. *See also* Apple
Johnson & Johnson crisis, 96

Kelleher, Herb, 51
Kelley, Tom, 73–74
Kelly, Gary C., 52
Kelly, Jim, 104–5
Kindle reader (Amazon), 31–32, 81–82, 85
Klapmeier, Alan, 4, 26–33. *See also* Cirrus Aviation
Klein, John, 42, 89–90. *See also* Cognizant Technology Solutions
Koch, Jim: letting go, for gaining control by, 41; process decisions by, 5, 35–39, 41. *See also* Boston Beer Company; Samuel Adams beer

Lennox, Annie, 79
Letting go, for gaining control, 40–41
Limit-setting, for reaching higher goals, 39–40
LinkedIn: distinctions from Facebook, 16; empowerment by, 4, 11, 16–17, 30; universality of, 4, 15–17
Littman, Jonathan, 73–74
London Evening Standard newspaper, 80

Machiavelli, Niccolo, 25
Made to Stick: Why Some Ideas Survive and Others Die (Chip and Dan Heath), 47
Madonna, 79

Manallack, Stephen, 93
Martin, Chris, 78
Mastering the Rockefeller Habits (Harnish), 94
McDonald's fast food chain, 39–40
Meditation for employees, 7, 92–94
MySpace, 14

Needle in a Haystack group (Facebook), 14
Netflix (DVD company), 5; banishing small thinking by, 7, 67–68; detached reflection by, 88–89; process decisions by, 44–45
Netscape, 87
Never Eat Alone (Ferrazzi), 93
Newmark, Craig, 7, 76–77. *See also* Craigslist
Nonprocess processes, 45–47
Nook reader (Barnes & Noble), 81
Nye, Dan, 15–17. *See also* LinkedIn

Obsession with customers, 31–33
Oldenburg, Ray, 19
Omidyar, Pierre, 18
Ozzie, Ray, 100

Page, Larry, 11, 71–73
Peanut Butter Manifesto story, 94
Pittinsky, Matthew, 23–26, 31. *See also* Blackboard software company
"The Power of Time Off" talk (Sagmeister), 92
Proactive inaction strategy, 7–8, 86
Process decisions, 35–47; of Boston Beer, Jim Koch, 35–39; of Chipotle Grill, Steve Ells, 5, 35–39; of Cognizant Technologies, D'Souza, 5, 8, 41–44; and customers, 5, 37–44, 46; described, 5; of Netflix, Reed Hastings, 5, 44–45; nonprocess processes, 45–47; questions for owners and managers, 108; representation by Shiva, 35; of Zappos, 40–41
Putnam, Robert, 13

Quicken software, 69–71, 98–100

Reinvention, 95–105; and customers, 8, 95–104; by Dell, 8, 95–97; described, 8; by FedEx, 97; by Hilti Fleet Management, 8, 97–98; by Intuit/Quickbooks, 98–100; by Microsoft, 100–101; questions for owners and managers, 110; by Radio Shack, 97; representation by Shiva, 95; by Starbucks, 97; by United Parcel Service, 101–5
Risk-blindness: of Alan Klapmeier, 26; of Michael Chasen, 25
Robinson, Peter, 80
Rose, Charlie, 81–82

Sagmeister, Stefan, 92
Samuel Adams beer. See Boston Beer Company; Koch, Jim
Schroeder, Kathy, 98–99
Schultz, Howard, 19
Schwab, Charles R., 29–31
Search technology, 11, 13. See also Google
Sezmi company, 91
Shape-shifting by United Parcel Service, 103–4
Shiva symbolism: appetite for destruction representation, 75; banishing small thinking representation, 63; book chapter titles relation to, 2; detachment representation, 85; fearlessness representation, 23; irreverence representation, 49; process representation, 35; reinvention representation, 95; universality representation, 11
Smith, Fred, 103
Social networking. See Facebook; MySpace
Sony Reader, 81
Southwest Airlines: creativity valued at, 62; employee happiness at, 51–52; individuality honored at, 61;

irreverence/transformative idea of, 49–52; self-reflective ideas by, 51; workforce empowerment, 5–6
Spice Girls, 79
Springfield Remanufacturing Corp. (SRC): management turnaround strategies, 58; toleration of mistakes at, 61; utilization of employee ideas, 60; workplace transformation at, 59. See also Stack, Jack
Stack, Jack: empowerment of employees, 6, 57; "Great Game of Business" of, 57, 59; quantitative management style, 58; transformation of SRC, 58–59. See also Springfield Remanufacturing Corp.
Starbucks: as created "third place," 19–21; "escape" sold by, 4, 12; universality of, 4
Stock market. See Schwab, Charles R.
Supply Chain Solutions (SCS), 101
Swasey, Steve, 88
Swinmurn, Nick, 53. See also Zappos (online shoe retailer)

Taylor, Suzanne, 98–99
Ten Faces of Innovation: IDEO's Strategies for Defeating the Devil's Advocate and Driving Creativity throughout Your Organization (Kelley & Littman), 73–74
Think Week policy (of Bill Gates), 7, 85, 87
"Third place" concept, 19–21
Timing's role in success: appetite for destruction and, 7; fearlessness and, 29; of Jeff Bezos, 65; in universal companies, 21

Underwood, Carrie, 78
"Unfriend" as verb of the year, 14
United Parcel Service (UPS), 101–5
Universality, 11–21; and customers, 12; description, 3–4, 12; of eBay, 12, 17–19; ephemeral quality of,

13; of Facebook, 14–15; of Google, 4, 11; quality of companies tapping into, 12, 13; questions for owners and managers, 107–8; representation by Shiva, 11
Universal Music UK, 79

Vipassana meditation, 93

Washington Post advertising rates, 76
Welch, Jack, 99
What Would Google Do? (Jarvis), 73, 76
Wieden, Dan, 62
Wieden+Kennedy advertising agency, 62
Wiser, Phil, 91
Wright, Laura, 52

Yahoo, 11

Zappos (online shoe retailer), 5, 6; call center excellence, 54, 56; creativity valued at, 62; customer-centric return policy, 54–55; customer happiness with, 57; employee incentives, 56; employee "zany" events, 52–53; individuality honored at, 61; irreverence by, 5, 6, 52–57, 62; letting go, for gaining control by, 40–41; "people-people" hired by, 55; Ten Commandments of, 53, 56; toleration of mistakes at, 61; training program, 55–56. *See also* Hsieh, Tony; Swinmurn, Nick
Zuckerberg, Mark, 14–15. *See also* Facebook

About the Author

T. D. KLEIN is an investor, author, and speaker who has spent his career focusing on transformative companies. He is founder and managing partner of Legend Ventures, LLC, and has invested in over 80 entrepreneurial enterprises in media and technology. His published works include *East of Wall Street*. He is a frequent speaker on capital formation and entrepreneurship. He has been quoted in the *Associated Press*, *Boston Globe*, and several other publications. Klein is a member of the Young Presidents Organization (YPO) and is the founder and chairman of YPO's global Raising Capital seminar, the leading capital formation educational program for YPO worldwide. He holds a BBA from the University of Texas and an MBA from Harvard University.